D0361089

THROUGH
A GLASS
DARKLY

THROUGH A GLASS DARKLY

A Spiritual Psychology of Faith

Mary Jo Meadow

A Crossroad Book
The Crossroad Publishing Company
New York

1996

The Crossroad Publishing Company
370 Lexington Avenue, New York, NY 10017

Copyright © 1996 by Mary Jo Meadow

All rights reserved. No part of this book may be reproduced, stored in a
retrieval system, or transmitted, in any form or by any means, electronic,
mechanical, photocopying, recording, or otherwise, without the written
permission of The Crossroad Publishing Company.

Printed in the United States of America

Library of Congress Cataloging-in-Publication Data
Meadow, Mary Jo, 1936–
    Through a glass darkly : a spiritual psychology of faith / Mary Jo
Meadow.
        p. cm.
    Includes bibliographical references.
    ISBN 0-8245-1510-2 (pb)
    1. Faith — Psychology. 2. Faith development. 3. Psychology,
Religious. I. Title.
BT771.2.M43 1995
234'.2 — dc20
                                                            95-13753
                                                            CIP

This book is gratefully dedicated to
Paul Meier Wiesner,
Patrick Keating,
the late Charles Morrissey, o.m.i.,
and Kevin Culligan, o.c.d.

WE SEE NOW THROUGH A GLASS DARKLY,
BUT THEN WE SHALL SEE FACE TO FACE.
— I CORINTHIANS 13:12

CONTENTS

PREFACE   11

Part I
THE GROUNDWORK
FOR EXAMINING FAITH

1. THE WRONG QUESTIONS:
   On God, Religions, and Creeds   21

2. CONCEPTS AND REALITY:
   Distinguishing Thought and Experience   28

3. SYMBOL, RITUAL, MYTH, METAPHOR:
   The Language of Religion   36

4. FAITH'S PLACES OF REFUGE:
   Teacher, Teachings, and Community   44

Part II
PROBLEMS IN
UNDERSTANDING FAITH

5. FAITH IS NOT WHAT YOU BELIEVE:
   Freedom from Opinions   53

6. FAITH IS NOT FEELING SURE:
   The Problem of Religious Certainty   61

7. FAITH IS NOT BLIND:
   The Need for Hard Questions   68

8. FAITH IS NOT NARROW:
   The Perversions of Faith   75

9. FAITH IS NOT EXCLUSIVE:
   Toward Universal Perspectives   83

Part III
A FAITH THAT
SERVES WELL

10. FAITH IS A CHOICE:
    Having It "Be So"   93

11. FAITH IS A CONFIDENT EXPERIMENT:
    "Gambling" with Our Lives   101

12. FAITH IS SOMETIMES DIFFICULT:
    Doubt, Wavering, and Not-Knowing   108

13. FAITH IS A DARKNESS:
    Embracing the Unknown   116

14. FAITH IS A DYNAMIC PROCESS:
    Coming Home to God   123

POSTSCRIPT   131

NOTES   137

Preface

Have you ever thought, "I must have lost my faith," or "My faith is not what it should be"? This book is for everyone who has. It is for all who blame themselves for being unable to feel certain about religious stories and ideas. It is also for people who find others concerned about their faith, others who think they lack "proper" faith and who want to convert them. Finally, anyone interested in exploring this deeply personal and value-laden aspect of human experience will find here ideas to ponder, understandings to consider.

Anguish over faith spurred in me a continuing interest in understanding faith. For several bleak years in my early twenties, I was convinced that I had "lost my faith." Steeped in the attitude that faith is a hothouse flower that cannot withstand normal climates, I "knew" that I must have done something horribly wrong to cause this sad state. I was not helped by several willing priests who quickly agreed with my assessment, suggesting that I carefully examine myself to see where and how I had erred.

Over the years, I have realized that I am not alone in such suffering. As I resolved my own difficulties, I found others in similar crises coming to me for help. Their stories have convinced me that the problem lies not in their faith, but in faulty understandings of faith. I once held similar unfortunate notions.

TO UNDERSTAND THIS BOOK

We begin with several disclaimers. I write from my own center and simply try to be honest. What understanding I have comes from my own experiences and those that others have shared with me. It is fed by Eastern as well as Western springs, as I have done intensive spiritual practice in several traditions. It is also fed by my training as a personality and clinical psychologist, specializing in understanding religious behavior. My conclusions "make sense" within these contexts, but I would never insist that they make up the best or only way to understand faith. I know only that these approaches to faith have helped both me and others in pain with whom I have shared them.

This book is not an exhaustive scholarly work. My main intent is to serve the spiritual needs of readers by expanding their horizons and presenting faith as a chosen commitment. I cite only scholars whose work helped me develop my thought. Others who have written on faith, many of them well received, are not included since I am not trying to summarize all opinion on the topic.

I also do not write to satisfy the wide range of theologians, or to conform my opinions to orthodox thinking. I attack common understandings that have caused people unnecessary suffering. In doing this, I deal with concerns that have entered the minds of many people. Religious conditioning often makes us consider some thoughts too scary to articulate or too dangerous to acknowledge. I hope this book comforts those who have felt that they alone had such thoughts.

This book is an interfaith dialogue. Being religious once meant knowing just one tradition. Today we live in a different world. Those whose faith cannot acknowledge the value of other traditions will find their own tradition discounted by thoughtful people. Scholarship also has shed new light on how we understand such religious figures as the Buddha and the Christ.

This book is also psychological, for we function as psychological beings. It argues for experientially based understandings of faith. It holds that the most honest, helpful, and effective faith must be based on what is common to all the great traditions that have withstood the test of time.

A word about language. When possible to do so without distorting passages, I have corrected sexist language in authors I quote. Sometimes, however, I have let such language stand rather than interrupt the flow of the quotation with an intrusive change. To pre-

serve a smoothly reading text, I have not indicated minor deletions
that do not change meaning when I cite other authors. The spelling
has been changed to standard American usage when authors who
spell according to British English are cited.

ON FAITH AND BELIEF

Faith has been considered many different ways across religions and
history. This book does not deny that fact, but suggests taking a good
hard look at understandings of faith that seem less adequate and
helpful than others. Many of these derive from the Mediterranean
mind — from Greek philosophy and Roman law, which often seem
inept vehicles for contemporary people's thought.

A major thesis of this work is that Western Christianity currently
holds some ways of looking at faith that cause needless anguish. The
problems have been building over time and, without clearly seeing them, we have accepted without complaint understandings of
faith far different from those of early Christians. The great traditions
of the East have recognized serious problems in such understandings. I hope that exploring these issues — sometimes seeing ourselves
through Eastern eyes — will bring some solace and understanding to
confused or suffering readers.

People use the word "belief" to denote both faith and opinions. In
common usage people even take "belief" to be *synonymous* with both
faith and also various kinds of opinions. I hold that neither of these
understandings is our best use of the word "belief." Religious belief
is neither faith nor simple opinion. In some ways, it stands between
the two. Like opinion, it is a conceptual activity. Because it refers to
any given tradition's verbal formulation of its faith, belief is related
to faith. Religious beliefs are attempts to grasp the object of faith in
a way that can be communicated.

Ideally, any religious belief flows from prior faith experience and is
held with willingness to revise it as seems appropriate, when further
experience calls for a different formulation. When religious beliefs
lack solid experiential grounding, they are easily apt to degenerate
into simple opinions. Some people's "faith" consists only of strongly
held opinions. They often cling to such opinions in a manner anti-

thetical to the openness to truth that faith requires. Any belief not rooted in experience is usually both fragile and overvalued.

Faith itself is much broader than religious beliefs. It can support many different belief systems. We greatly diminish faith when we hold that it must or can be defined only in the terminology of one tradition, in the words or formulas that a particular tradition has chosen to express its faith. Deep faith allows us to see that many different faith-full beliefs, formulations of truth, are possible — some more and some less adequate than others. "All these phrases are just translations into a given language and understandable in a given tradition, of something that outsoars all utterance."[1]

Because the word "belief" is used in many different ways, it presents special problems in this book. We say both "I believe in God" and "I believe it will rain tomorrow." How helpful the archaic word "opine" would be to express opinions: "I opine it will rain tomorrow"! Lacking "opine," we must use "believe" and "belief" to cover different types of conceptualizing — including blind opinion, reasoned considerations, and religious belief.

When the context does not make it obvious, I designate "religious belief" when I refer to conceptual formulations of faith in this book. I use the more generic "belief" to refer to the outcome of both religious believing and holding opinions. I *never* use "belief" as synonymous with faith, for a major thesis of this book is that such usage creates serious problems.

RESOURCES FOR THIS BOOK

Although this book draws from the academic psychology of religion, people's faith experience forms its basis. Its being about experience makes it a much deeper psychology than any merely academic discussion could be. Most of the psychologists quoted speak from their own soul experience, from their personal grappling with faith issues. Some examples from the author's experiences also illustrate points.

In talking about soul experience, this book truly studies the *psyche* as soul, the original meaning of the word. This meaning goes far deeper into our beings than the understandings of contemporary psychology. Ultimately we all must fall back on our own soul experience. This may be accepting what other people say to us about something — which is also an experience, muddling through to our own conclusions, or seeing in sudden flashes of insight. This book addresses all these faith experiences.

In addition to psychology, this book discusses Christian faith with insights from Theravadan Buddhism and the Hindu schools of *ashtanga* yoga and Vedanta, the latter mainly as explained by Sri Aurobindo. It occasionally draws from several other traditions. It calls upon the wisdom of these non-Christian traditions to illuminate Christian blind spots and problematic stances. The discussion is supported by the author's years of intensive spiritual practice in Christian, Hindu, and Buddhist faith stances.

SOME MENTORS

Nobody's thought stands simply by itself. Some people have greatly influenced my understanding of faith. You find them cited throughout this book. Often an end note directs you to where one of them discusses the point being made. Now I briefly introduce them.

First, some saints. Vedantic mystic Sri Aurobindo, one of the great lights of twentieth-century India, was educated in England. He fought for India's independence before adopting the life of a yogi and giving us spiritual disciplines and understandings suitable for contemporary persons. Sixteenth-century Spanish Christian mystic and Carmelite friar St. John of the Cross was my first great teacher. He has been named a Doctor of the Catholic Church, which affirms that his teachings are trustworthy doctrine. Benedictine monk Henri Le Saux went to India to study and practice Vedanta. He helped found an Indian style Benedictine ashram and took the Indian renunciate name of Abhishiktananda, "he who takes his delight in the Christ."

Psychologists as well as holy people have been important. Turn-of-the-century figure William James suffered torments over religious faith and finally adopted transcendentalist views. He had a keen eye for detecting religious perversions. At mid-century Gordon Allport was a devout Protestant who also studied the failure of the religious intent. Menninger Clinic's Paul Pruyser had a special interest in faith and unbelief.

Several scholars of religious studies are also key figures. American Wilfred Cantwell Smith, Protestant, Harvard professor, and scholar of Islam, wrote penetratingly about faith, belief, and reason. Sarvepalli Radhakrishnan, former vice-president of India, has taught in both the United States and England. Catholic priest-scholar Raimundo Panikkar was born of an East-West marriage.

Other key figures, cited less frequently, include St. Thomas Aquinas, longshoreman-philosopher Eric Hoffer, Christian scripture scholar and biblical translator J. B. Phillips, and psychologists Abraham Maslow and Erich Fromm. The text also includes occasional insights from various other mystics, scholars, and ordinary people of faith.

PLAN OF THIS BOOK

Overall, this book looks at the bases of faith, what happens inside faith, and at faith's outcomes. It has three main sections. The first part lays the groundwork for examining faith, looking at faith questions and religious language.

The second part studies understandings of faith that appear to be unworkable. When these chapters say that "faith is not...," they are claiming that these ways of viewing faith seem unsatisfactory. Such stances have outlived whatever usefulness they may ever have had. The third section discusses what faith most helpfully *is*. It argues that helpful faith is a choice, a chosen risk, often has difficult features, and is not a "thing" but a living process.

ACKNOWLEDGMENTS

Some chapters in this book were developed from lecture materials on faith prepared and presented for Notre Dame University, Australia. I thank the university for inviting my work, and also Fr. Douglas Conlan of the Perth archdiocese in Western Australia for arranging for my visits, lectures, and retreats there.

Teachers and spiritual friends in both Eastern and Western faith traditions have supported both my own faith life and my work. I have acknowledged Buddhist teachers elsewhere.[2] Several teachers in both the *ashtanga* yoga and Vedantic aspects of the Hindu tradition have also been very helpful; they will be thanked in more detail in future works.

In this book, I want especially to mention the support of several Christian helpers. Patrick Keating, then a Dominican priest, first showed me alternative ways to understand faith when I was drowning in dysfunctional interpretations. My Carmelite colleagues in retreat work and in writing, Fathers Kevin Culligan and Daniel Chowning, have also helped and supported me over the years.[3] The life of the late Charles Morrissey, O.M.I., was a very beautiful example for me. Three Dominican friars — Hillary Freeman, Larry Lux, and Richard Daniel — and two Jesuits — Martin Hasting and Sal Briffa — also helped importantly at particular times.

People who have come to me with their faith issues have greatly increased my understanding. So also members of spiritual groups in which I participate. Several people have read and made helpful comments on the manuscript in various stages of preparation — Kevin Culligan, Jeanne and Vera Epp, and Leo and Bertie Holley. Kevin and Jeanne were especially helpful — Kevin in keeping me factually accurate, and Jeanne grammatically so. Although I have incorporated many of their suggestions, I remain responsible for the final form of the book. I am grateful to all of the people named for their part in making this book possible.

Finally, I thank Michael Leach of Crossroad Publishing for his continuing interest in my work. I also thank my editor at Crossroad, John Eagleson, for help in finishing work on this manuscript.

DEDICATION

This book is dedicated to four men I have called "father." As a worthy antagonist who holds many positions that I abhor, it is first dedicated lovingly to my biological father, Paul Meier Wiesner. Our disagreements over faith have forced me to a much more careful examination of faith than I would otherwise have undertaken. In gratitude for his being my first important spiritual teacher and first pointing the way out of narrow understandings of faith, it is dedicated to Patrick Keating. Because he was an inspiring example of the life of faith well lived, it is dedicated to the late Charles Morrissey, O.M.I. Finally, in gratitude for our clarifying discussions on faith, it is dedicated to friend and colleague Kevin Culligan, O.C.D.

Part I

THE GROUNDWORK FOR EXAMINING FAITH

Chapter 1

THE WRONG QUESTIONS

ON GOD, RELIGIONS, AND CREEDS

Your God is too small.
— J. B. Phillips[1]

"Does God exist?" "Is there a God?" So many people agonize over such questions! The mental anguish of feeling "bad" or "wrong" for doubting is only the beginning of the suffering these questions cause. Answering the question contrary to common belief has even been dangerous. People have fought and killed each other over holding different views.

The same is true of questions about religious institutions and their religious beliefs. "Is there one true religion?" and "Are there certain dogmas that must be believed?" also cause many problems. Some questions *are* important to ask, but not any of these. Such unnecessary questions may even harm the life of faith. This chapter suggests ways of dealing with these questions that at first glimpse may seem frightening. Later chapters will further discuss all issues raised.

Here are two experiences that highlight the interior suffering caused by wrong ideas about faith. Swiss psychiatrist Carl Jung was outraged over the religious struggles of his clergyman father. Jung complained that all his father's prayer was begging for "faith" — that is, to make his mind think about God in church-approved ways. Jung said bitterly that his father had given his whole life to the church, whose dogmatic insistence then made him incapable of any genuine religious experience. Trying to feel certain about orthodox positions

21

consumed all his father's energy, and he was not free to see how God might come to him personally.[2]

In my youth I berated myself because I could not believe as parents, priests, and teaching sisters taught me I ought to believe — hold the right ideas with convinced certainty. I became quite sure that I must have done something horribly wrong to "lose my faith." No shortage of "helpful" priests either concurred with this judgment or advised me simply to trust in God so that I could again feel certain about what was true. I was well into my twenties before I found a priest wise enough to explain that faith is not feeling certain about religious notions, but rather a strong enough desire for God to spend one's entire life seeking God with all one's heart.

THE GOD QUESTION

The wrong question. Consider it possible that "Is there a God?" is the wrong question. Obviously God "ex-ists" — stands out or apart from that which is "other" — in the many forms that various religious traditions have celebrated for millennia. Different cultures each affirm their own notions of what the word "God" means to them in concepts that are very dear to the group delineating them. The characteristics of God defined by any one group are not the only possible beliefs that can be "true" of God. Also, some cultures say things about God that others find unacceptable.

When people ask "Does God exist?" they almost always have in mind some limited understanding of God. Most commonly, it is their own culture's majority opinion. Asking this question in various cultures is thus asking something quite different in each, although the same word "God" is used. If someone answers, "Yes, God exists," but obviously understands the words differently, the "true believer" finds this unsatisfactory.

Many people consider it very important that their understanding of God be the "highest," "real," or "correct" one. Questioning their beliefs frightens people whose security rests in thinking that their ideas completely define reality. They do not realize that any words or images used to depict God are only products of human thought and are *not* what we try to designate with them. Doctor of the Church

St. John of the Cross taught that any idea *about* God is *not* God.[3] Doctor of the Church St. Thomas Aquinas said that "the believer's act does not terminate in the propositions, but in the realities."[4]

Faulty understandings of God. J. B. Phillips's delightful book *Your God Is Too Small* excellently outlined many of the inadequate God-understandings Christian people have held. Here is his instructive list: resident policeman, parental hangover, grand old man, meek-and-mild, absolute perfection, heavenly bosom, God-in-a-box, managing director, second-hand God, perennial grievance, pale Galilean, and projected image.[5]

Phillips argued that many people today live without faith because their adult minds "have not found a God big enough to 'account for' life, big enough to 'fit in with' the new scientific age, big enough to command their highest admiration and respect, and consequently their willing co-operation."[6] Too many people rest the God-question upon images that are too small and consequently throw out the entire question because they cannot shape it appropriately.

An alternative question. If "Does God exist?" is the wrong question, what is a correct one? Let me recommend "What is the nature of the Ultimate Reality?" Or, "What is the ultimate nature of Reality?" These collapse into one question, which we can also word in various ways. "What is that beyond which there can be nothing higher?" "Pushed to the furthest end, what reality is the last or ultimate or most basic one?" These wordings make possible seeking an answer through spiritual practice, without closing off any options.

Rephrased in religious terms, the question becomes "What is God like?" Immediately, some protest that they already know the answer. They usually then cite some scripture or give their own religious group's officially sanctioned answer. Again — words, ideas, concepts! Not something they *know* from personal experience. They simply parrot someone else's answer to the question instead of doing spiritual practice to see for themselves.

Some people even *define* faith as accepting another person's answer — usually the view of someone who claims to speak infallibly about God. Across history, many figures have made such a claim, with varying degrees of credibility. Accepting someone else's answer may work fine as a starting hypothesis. How sad if it ends there! Re-

member! Your idea about God — or anybody else's — is *not* God.
We will say much more about this later, but it comes down to this:
do you want an idea or do you want God? For now, let the question become: of the many ways that we can consider God, which at
this time offers me the best way to arrive at experiential knowledge
of God?

THE CHURCH QUESTION

We discuss here the church as religious institution, for it is institutions — their leaders and unquestioning followers — that make
the claims that bind people. Chapter 4 discusses church as the
community of seekers.

Exclusive claims and institutional power. The new Catholic catechism explains that "it is through the Church that we receive
faith."[7] Although the broader church community commonly first offers us faith, the institutional church usually carefully monitors what
is taught. Religious institutions seem to be a "necessary evil" when
it comes to faith. They help transmit spiritual truths, but often limit
seekers' perspectives in ways that block spiritual growth and obscure
spiritual truths.

All human institutions work to perpetuate themselves once they
exist. Churches are no exception. Church leaders are usually conser-
vative elements in religion. A shift in loyalty, from the faith vision
of the founder to the organizational structure built on that vision,
commonly occurs in people who seek or obtain positions of power
in any church.[8] Perpetuating an institution is easiest when most ad-
herents simply say "yes" and question no further. An Eastern scholar
noted that so long as religions conform to comfortable worldly standards and support the established order, "those who revolt against
such practices are the truly religious people."[9]

Since they cannot easily control those who have seen for themselves, religions tend to persecute their seers and mystics while still
alive and revere them only after they are safely dead. Having direct
experience of God and spiritual realities confers a great freedom on
mystics. They realize that institutions cannot command God. The
tyranny of such punishments as "silencing," excommunication, be-

ing pronounced *anathema*, does not move mystics. They know that whatever words an institution pronounces over them have no effect on their relationship with God, but only on church leaders' perception of it.

The catechism cites as "external proofs" of the church's mediation of revelation "the miracles of Christ and the saints, prophecies, the Church's growth and holiness, and her fruitfulness and stability."[10] Such arguing does not acknowledge that many people do not so perceive the church. When used to claim a unique role, it also fails to consider the miracles of the Buddha, other great teachers, and their followers. It discounts other traditions' prophecies;[11] and growth, holiness, fruitfulness, and stability in various other traditions.

Evaluating exclusive claims. Is there only one way to God? Must we adhere to any one tradition to reach our final end with God? Many churches argue that this is so and that *they* are the needed tradition, for this fosters a dependency on them that ensures their perpetuation. Often "churches give the outsider the impression that God works almost exclusively through the machinery they have erected and, what is worse, damns all other machinery which does not bear their label."[12] Holding that one institution exclusively speaks for God is just another belief to evaluate. The Gospel of Matthew seems clearly to indicate that Jesus had no intention of having such structures erected in his name.[13] Read his exchanges with the Pharisees![14]

Religious institutions are prone to grandiosity. We should take any tradition that sets itself up as apart from and superior to others "with a grain of salt." Just because particular ways of understanding the Ultimate Mysteries have proven helpful for some in the past, that does not make them the best or only way for all people at all times. Let the question become: of all the worthy paths that have brought people to God, which is or are the best for me at this time?

THE CREED QUESTION

Hearing the message. "Faith comes from hearing the message" (Romans 10:17); however, we hear many different messages. Much that we hear does not deserve our faith. Our traditions give us the hearing, but we must constantly evaluate what they offer us. We must especially look at the packaging in which religious truths come, realizing that the packaging is *not* the truth itself. We must also stay able to hear; to hear, we must realize that we do not already have all the answers.

Vedanta says we first hear of a teaching from scriptures or a teacher. We should ponder it to understand it. Finally, we meditate to see the truth of it for ourselves.[15] Buddhist scriptures say similarly. "One having faith draws near; gives ear and hears *Dhamma*[16] and tests the meaning. Weighing it all up, [one] strives; being resolute [one] realizes the highest truth itself and sees it in all its detail by means of wisdom."[17]

From Hindu yoga we have: "Religious truths are not mere dogmas but facts made visible by an inner light."[18] We receive the inner light not from the words given us by others, but from our own work with them. Once we have "seen" for ourselves, alternative ways of wording truths may work better for us.[19]

These venerable Eastern traditions are saying that a particular teaching first comes by way of the senses. If it attracts us, we begin to explore and seek out a teacher. The teacher, though, is just a means. We must start practicing what we are taught to test and realize its wisdom. In these traditions, hearing is but the first step and does not give us final and complete truth and understanding. Ultimately we are called to spiritual practice, to see for ourselves the truth that lies behind the vehicles in which it is given.

How creeds work. Creeds or other formulations of religious beliefs are ways in which traditions try to express conceptually the faith vision that has guided them. Unfortunately, by the time a tradition formally organizes its understandings, it has usually already lost its inwardness and become controlled by a church structure. One psychologist said this happens when a faith community articulates and packages their understandings "to make the revelation available to the masses."[20]

We tend to overvalue, sometimes even idolize, the beliefs that state our faith. When people live in a homogeneous community, "most never notice the tension between faith and belief. They look on dogmas, which are simply authoritative formulations of belief, almost as if they were faith itself, half-forgetting that they are dogmas of faith."[21] This makes helpful revision difficult and can lead a group to want to force its own ways of formulating truth on other people.

Religious words are meant to be sacred symbols. To work as such, a symbol must meet criteria. "First, it is sacred; and second, it is therefore translucent."[22] To see if it can function sacredly for us, we must ask just how well any particular form represents our spiritual understanding.[23] Words also can be living or dead. When some die for us, we must "let the dead bury their own dead" (Matthew 8:21). This does not mean that what the words once signified has necessarily ceased to have value in itself; we may find new and better words to express it.

We must be open to new sacred symbols, verbal and otherwise. We can find other words, other symbols, that reawaken us to the reality that the symbol embodies. Sometimes people make changes that do not help them. The great Indian sage Sri Aurobindo warned that reilluminating, rather than destroying, old forms is usually best. Where destruction is necessary, the new forms should be richer and purified by spiritual insight rather than rational arguments.[24]

At recent spiritual conferences, women prayed to God as Sophia, the feminine figure of Holy Wisdom who appears in the Hebrew Bible. Such restructuring of symbols can keep alive faith that would die if it remained confined to formulations that have lost any adequacy they once had. Let the question become, "Which ways of formulating my faith are currently helpful to me — deepen my faith and lead me to God — and which need to be replaced?"

Chapter 2

CONCEPTS AND REALITY

DISTINGUISHING THOUGHT AND EXPERIENCE

Belief must bear *directly* upon the reality of God, not upon words or upon concepts. God reveals himself, not words about or concepts of himself.

— Leslie Dewart[1]

Think of an apple — the size, shape, smell, color, touch of it. Now bite into it, taste the sweet juice, chew the pulp, swallow it. You cannot really do this because your image of the apple is only a thought; it is not really an apple. If you spend all your time playing with images of apples, you will never actually taste a real apple.

How do we get so trapped in thoughts that we often find ourselves unable to taste the realities to which they point? The problem is how we interpret experiences. We translate them into concepts or ideas and then treat these mental products as if they were the real event. Many people even take such notions to *be* their faith. They choose the idea of apple over the apple itself.

UNDERSTANDING CONCEPTS

Experience and theology. William James wrote to a friend about this difference. "I have set myself two main goals: to defend experience rather than philosophy as the backbone of religion and to show that, although many manifestations of it may have been absurd, religion is still [our] most important endeavor."[2] James saw the futility of trying to comprehend the goal of religion with the mind alone. India's Sri Aurobindo said likewise: "If you persist in asking intellectual questions about that which is beyond the intellect, you will go on forever."[3] Such persistence is a common cause of James's "absurd manifestations."

"To defend experience rather than philosophy as the backbone of religion...." James emphasized what comes *before* we verbally rework our experiences, codify them, and formulate them into creeds and belief statements. When we stay trapped in intellectual meandering, we never truly come to know anything by direct experience. Many mental machinations that pass for religion were very distasteful to James.

He made a salty assessment of theologians: "What is their deduction of metaphysical attributes of God but a shuffling and matching of pedantic dictionary adjectives. The metaphysical monster which they offer to our worship is an absolutely worthless invention of the scholarly mind."[4]

Self-concepts and religion. We human beings usually define and value ourselves by comparing ourselves with other people. We develop concepts to describe ourselves, faith, family, and country, and then think these define the "right" way to be. Often these self-understandings remain unevaluated and poorly understood.

We also set ourselves strongly against others' self-identity with little awareness of what that is. Our sense of who "we" are rests on seeing how "we" are different from and better than other people — outsiders, barbarians, pagans, infidels, savages, heretics, sinners, aliens, and primitives. This leaves us with a shaky identity we must work hard to defend.[5]

Religious institutions feed this comparing. History shows that they often support warfare and injustice when the "right" people with the "right" beliefs encounter those with differing opinions. They frequently present distorted understandings of others. "For every belief we are taught to love, we are taught to hate or despise several alternative beliefs. It takes considerable fortitude and acumen to avoid exposure to such influences or to overcome their effects."[6] Yet we and our churches continue to define self and faith in such divisive ways.

DISTINGUISHING CONCEPTS AND REALITY

Here are some stories to help distinguish concepts from real experience. Such understanding begins our freedom from the tyranny of concepts.

Conviction of sin. A "born-again" Christian told me that Jesus Christ convicted him of sin in his heart. When I asked him what experience he was interpreting this way, he just repeated that Jesus Christ convicted him of sin in his heart. I then described an experience I had in Buddhist meditation practice.

The man sitting in front of me kept shifting position and moving around, apparently struggling with pain. An odd sort of delight arose in me, and then I remembered that this man had earlier annoyed me. In a flash, I realized that I was enjoying the discomfort of someone who had previously irked me. This was followed by hot, searing pain in my chest and disgust with myself. I judged myself to be vindictive and felt deep revulsion to so being. I also felt trapped in this emotional bondage and desired to be free of such. My cheeks burned with a deep sense of shame, and silent tears ran down my cheeks. Intense remorse flooded me.

I asked the "born-again" man if his experience was anything like mine. He was genuinely confused and insisted again that his experience was of being convicted of sin in his heart. He said that he was referring to a religious experience, while I was talking about feelings I had while doing a pagan practice. He just could not distinguish between what he actually experienced and the interpretation he added.

Academic jargon. Lest you think him especially dense, here is another story. At a Buddhist-Christian conference I read a paper comparing spiritual development in Buddhist *vipassana* (insight) meditation with teachings of St. John of the Cross.[7] One man commented that the parallels seemed very striking. However, he continued, one insolvable problem is the importance of grace in Christianity, for which "atheistic" Buddhism has no parallel. Inwardly sighing, I told him an anecdote I hoped would help.

My Buddhist teacher had emphasized that all must walk their own road, that nobody will do this work for us.[8] We must each apply ourselves to meditation to purify our minds. I became concerned because my experience greatly differed from this teaching. I told him, "I have never felt more carried in my entire life." He smiled and said, "Oh, yes, once you start to experience the unfolding of the *Dharma*,[9] they are both true." I asked my conference questioner, "What difference does it make what we call it — grace or the unfolding of the *Dharma?* Most Christians would call feeling carried 'grace.'" From the look on his face I sensed that he did not understand what I was saying.

Although most Christians would consider both my experiences "grace" within a Christian context, these men could not recognize them as such because I did not use Christian concepts. This inability suggests that they are living entirely too much in concepts, beliefs, and ideas rather than in direct faith experience. Many of us do this.

HOW WE MAINTAIN BELIEFS

Certain mental processes keep us holding on to beliefs. None of these factors that so control our thinking constitutes faith. They simply affect views and powerfully shape our understandings of self, life, others, and religious truths.

Attribution. The human mind likes to make sense of things; we are meaning-makers. We want to label, interpret, and understand what happens. Attributions are the causes we use to explain events. We might attribute them to chance, luck, God, or personal characteristics like talent. We do this for both religious and other experiences.[10]

Religious testimonies are usually full of unfounded attributions. When faced with something otherwise unexplainable, saying that God made it happen is easy. Atypical or unexpected happenings may be called miracles. The more religious people are, the more likely they will find supernatural forces at work in any event. Unfortunately, we can develop elaborate interpretive frameworks with little or no factual basis.

Nothing is wrong about this natural function of the human mind, but we need to know when we are making attributions. Once we attribute cause, we find more and more confirming evidence to support our conclusions. Attributions thus strongly shape future interpretations by bending us to see things in certain ways. We tend to disregard disconfirming evidence and see only what supports our belief. Whenever alternative explanations of anything are possible, we choose one consistent with the preconceptions our attributions have created.

Explaining spiritual experience. Genuinely transcendent experience, loss of self-sense in spiritual experience, often brings invincible faith. Unfortunately, this faith usually becomes attached solely to specific interpretations found within our own religious tradition. These interpretations have only the inadequate tool of language to use. While many languages distinguish at least two types of knowing, English does not. Sorting out the difference between knowing propositions and first-hand experiential knowing is harder in English. We often try to reduce knowing by spiritual insight to something we can grasp with the reason.

Experiences that could really open or expand our perspectives turn constrictive when we confine them to pre-existing frameworks. Such faith rests in concepts or words rather than in God or the Ultimate Mystery. An antidote is to have spiritual experience in more than one tradition. Then we can see that only God, and not any particular set of interpretations, deserves our faith. Sri Aurobindo said that spiritual life begins with our first experience of God and develops as we know God in other ways.[11]

Cognitive dissonance. When any important belief — religious or other — clashes with disconfirming evidence, one feels a very unpleasant state of mind that psychologists call cognitive dissonance. When people have really invested themselves in a belief, which is common with religion, disconfirming evidence can be agonizing. They feel that anything would be better than letting go of a belief purchased at great cost or which they have held for a long time. To try to stop the pain of dashed hope, they ignore the disconfirmation if they can. Sometimes denying disconfirming evidence puts one grossly out of touch with reality.

Another common tactic when important beliefs are disconfirmed is aggressive proselytizing. One supports faltering belief by trying to get more people to agree with the position. Someone once said to me, "I never defended my religious beliefs more vigorously than when I was least sure of them." This strategy more deeply entrenches us in beliefs that might not be genuinely supportable but that we need badly enough that we will distort reality to keep.[12]

THE CONCEPT TRAP

Interpretation and reason. We constantly interpret experience; we must do so to survive in the material world. It helps us to understand that a red light means to stop and to conclude that this "thing" coming toward me is an angry dog. However, interpretation is virtually useless in spiritual practice and often causes great harm. Once we interpret, we run the risk of serious error. So long as we stay with bare experience, we are on firm ground.

A suitable role for reason regarding spiritual experience is discernment, which Buddhists call "wise consideration." We must examine the effects of particular experiences on us, so we know whether or not to leave ourselves "open" for more of the same kind of experience. This need not involve interpretation.

If I have a beautiful, warm feeling when praying, to say that God caused it is so easy. Some people might even argue that a person of faith *should* attribute it to God; mystics would say they are wrong. Although the experience itself is valid and comforting, interpretation is something extra. Somebody else might say that gremlins caused the feeling, that hormone levels in the body came into balance, or that the brain released a surge of endorphins, its natural narcotics.

The point is: interpretations obscure bare experience itself. This occurred with the man convicted of sin in his heart. He no longer knew what actually happened to him because he lived only in his interpretation of it. He just *could* be wrong!

Recent years have seen movement away from the tyranny of conceptual understanding. Sri Aurobindo said, "There has been a very noticeable revolt of the human mind against this sovereignty of the intellect, a dissatisfaction with the reason itself and its own limitations. Vaguely it is felt that there is some greater godhead than the reason."[13]

Changing nature of concepts. Concepts do not eternally "stay put" for us. Many small changes over a long period of time can bring radically changed meanings. Such changes have occurred with some words that are very important to faith. "In the early Christian church, the 'I do' [of] giving of themselves in full sincerity and in formal commitment is, more aptly, 'I set my heart.' The Latin word chosen for translation, '*credo,*' has as its primary meaning 'to entrust, to commit, to trust something to someone.' "[14]

Modern usage of the word "belief" connotes a cognitive rather than motivational activity. The Latin word that best describes this use is *opinio,* from which we get the word "opinion." *Credo* is the pledging of loyalty to truth, and "faith" (*fides*) is the loyalty itself. One should not use *credo* — usually translated "I believe" — to describe the position of people who know the truth but are not loyal to it.[15]

Scholar W. C. Smith humorously noted that now to say one believes in God means "so-and-so reports that the idea of God is part of the furniture of his mind."[16] But this English word had a different original meaning. Believing in something meant you held it dear, trusted it, esteemed it, loved it.[17] "The evidence is overwhelmingly conclusive that words such as *bilefe, blieve,* and the like designated allegiance, commitment, the placing of one's heart, choice — and not propositional constructs" in the Middle Ages.[18]

Some closing thoughts on concepts. The conclusion of high mystic St. John of the Cross is very simple: since God is transcendent, no human concept or understanding can adequately contain God. We can approach God directly only by letting go of our concepts *about* God.[19] Abhishiktananda deplored the importance of conceptual knowledge to Christianity, saying that "Greek intellectualism deeply influenced the development of Christian thought, so much so that at times rationalism tended to extinguish the sense of mystery."[20]

However the major church trends went, distinguishing between real experience and concepts about it has always been central to both the great Christian mystics and Eastern spirituality. Both explain that any words or images we have — of God or anything else — are simply not that reality itself. So thinking about anything, studying it conceptually, trying to grasp it intellectually — none of this gives us direct contact with the reality itself. We must empty out concepts, which get in the way of direct, true, experiential knowing. Walking in faith requires the emptiness of discarding all concepts that interfere with the direct experience of Truth.

Chapter 3

SYMBOL, RITUAL, MYTH, METAPHOR

THE LANGUAGE OF RELIGION

Faith is believing what you know ain't so.

— Mark Twain[1]

Faith is when you believe what nobody in their right mind would believe.

— Archie Bunker[2]

Many problems with faith come from improperly understanding religious language. Religious language is neither history nor science. Treating it as either seriously distorts it. Religious language uses analogies; it is symbolic, mythical, metaphorical. Rather than concretely depicting particular objects of experience, its words "stand for" other meanings.

Abhishiktananda remarked that "whatever [one] tries to think or say about God is inevitably marked with ignorance."[3] Metaphorical language helps us deal with such truths that we cannot directly grasp intellectually. Recall the story of Carl Jung's father given in chapter 1.[4] Understanding the mythic nature of religious language would have prevented much of his suffering.

When the poet lover could not adequately describe how beautiful his beloved was to him, he said, "My love is like a red, red rose." With the word "like," he clearly stated the analogy. In anal-

36

ogy, the meaning is partly the same as the literal meaning and partly different. Analogy abstracts out some connotations of a term, while discarding others. The poet's love is both like and not like a rose.

Had the poet said instead, "My love is a red, red rose," the meaning would be the same. Here he would have been speaking metaphorically, as both religion and poetry often do. We do this when we say "God is ruler," "God is father," and so on. Devotional Hinduism refers to God with a variety of relationship metaphors: parent, child, friend, lover, sovereign, and antagonist. We can relate to God through such images, but must always remember that they are not literal facts.

UNDERSTANDING MYTH AND SYMBOL

To understand religious language we must look behind the words for hidden meanings that we cannot easily grasp with concepts. Sacred objects, actions, and stories can also depict such meanings.

Symbol. Symbols are objects, images, or ideas that stand for something else. They appear not only in religion, but also in fairy tales, mythology, dreams, folklore, literature, psychotic thinking, art, and even everyday life. One psychologist, who called symbolic language "the forgotten language,"[5] described three types of symbols: conventional, accidental, and universal.

Everyday language uses conventional symbols. Words are just conventional symbols; they stand for something else — the objects they denote. Calling that four-legged being wandering around the house "cat" is symbolic. Spanish-speaking cultures use a different symbol — *gato* — to refer to the same creature. Conventional symbols can also be images, such as a painting or statue of a very northern European-looking man that we say depicts Jesus. Conventional symbols are arbitrary; they can be anything people agree to use. Religious artwork usually uses the ethnic features of the group producing it.

Accidental symbols also have no inherent connection with what they designate. They are usually unique to particular persons or groups — like "our song," which stands for the love between two people. Religions develop many accidental symbols with particular meanings for themselves, which are not symbolically important to anyone else. The cross stands for salvation to Christians, but is only a geometric figure to some people. Most sacramentals are accidental symbols.

Universal symbols have an intrinsic relationship with what they signify. They are based on the affinity between certain experiences and particular emotions or thoughts. Fire, water, a mountain, the sky, or a baby each tends to evoke similar deep reactions in people. Water universally stands for rebirth, cleansing, and purity. It is used in baptism rituals, but also by people with compulsive disorders who repeatedly wash their hands trying to eradicate unconscious guilt. Shakespeare understood symbolic acts in having Lady Macbeth compulsively try to wash away the guilt of murder. Religions easily take on universal symbols.

Symbol and sign. Some people call conventional symbols "signs" rather than "symbols" because they do directly denote their objects. They reserve the word "symbol" for situations that imply more than a direct and obvious meaning. True symbols touch us in deep, unconscious ways that defy any exact definition or explanation.

Religious people sometimes treat their tradition's accidental and universal symbols as concrete signs. Some even see the symbol as the reality itself. One might bathe a statue of the infant Jesus so that baby Jesus will not suffer from being dirty. Bathing the statue as a symbolic act of love would be a more mature use of symbol. Some Catholics still refuse to touch the eucharistic host, feeling that they would actually desecrate Jesus by doing so! Such people understand neither symbol nor the nature of the Christ's presence in the Eucharist.

SYMBOLIC ACTION AND THOUGHT

Myth. Myth does not mean falsehood, fantasy, or error. Calling something a myth means that it is a story, not literally true in itself, that points to deeper, hidden truths. Myths help us understand the world around us, provide for emotional expression and celebration in rituals, guide us through stages of life, and awaken our sense of awe and mystery.

In many ways, faith rests on myth. Myths open us to the truths to which they point. The new Catholic catechism says, "We do not believe in formulas, but in those realities they express, which faith allows us to touch."[6] Would that more religious people understood the propositions of faith in this way instead of taking them literally! Sri Aurobindo said, "The besetting sin of metaphysics [is] the tendency to battle in the clouds because it deals with words as if they were imperative facts instead of symbols which have to be brought back constantly to the sense of that which they represent."[7] The truths to which myth leads us do not rest in scientific demonstration, logical deduction, or historical fact. Joseph Campbell, a great scholar of mythology, defined myth as a story or "symbol that evokes and directs psychological energy."[8]

Some people read the Christian story of creation and the Garden of Eden as literal history. Others argue that we can deduce such beginnings since the human race had to start somewhere, and they find evolution rationally untenable. Some Christian scientists have even developed what they call "creation science" and have waged court battles to force its being taught as an alternative science to evolution.

What might this creation story, seen as myth, tell us? Perhaps that we are contingent beings, not capable of bringing about or sustaining our own existence. That behavior has consequences, that choices are important for future happiness. That self-importance is divisive and causes suffering. That a state of relatedness better than the way we usually live is possible. Reading the story this way does not do it injustice; this method searches for meanings far more important to our lives than whether the story is literally or historically true. Other religious traditions have similar myths that point to the same conclusions. We can celebrate the truths we agree upon rather than cling literally to any single story that embodies them.

Ritual. Since ritual deals with the unseen and unthinkable, it necessarily resorts to symbols. Some myths form the basis for reenactment rituals, such as the Jewish Passover or the Christian Eucharist. These let us see and reenact the great mysteries through concrete experiences, events, and objects taken to reflect them.

Sharing symbolic activity bonds a community and supports members' religious endeavor.

Sacrament is symbolic behavior that makes the holy tangible. The objects used and actions done represent much more than what meets the eye. The outsider sees someone eating a small wafer of bread, but the eating person sees union with the divine. Sacraments actually celebrate something that has already happened. They confirm choices made, rejoice over correcting mistakes, symbolize the presence of God, and so on. Sacraments point to our basic connection with all else that is. We can make daily activities — such as eating and showering, even breathing — sacramental in nature by being aware of how they show our connection with the world around us.

All worship and liturgical celebrations are symbols in action. People often perform them unthinkingly, simply accepting them as something they do each Sunday, and do not benefit from them as symbolic acts. Others actively participate in the symbol, reflecting on whatever richness they encounter. Sometimes symbolic actions lose their power to captivate attention and direct it to the holy. Although lax attentiveness is sometimes the problem, the ritual may have lost its inwardness and need to be replaced.

We can use ritual either rationally or irrationally. When someone becomes compulsive about doing the ritual in just the right way or becomes upset with any change in it, irrational elements have crept in. "One can always recognize the irrational ritual by the degree of fear produced by its violation in any manner."[9]

Rational ritual "expresses strivings which are recognized as valuable by the individual."[10] When we use ritual rationally, the symbols are sufficiently transparent that we realize that the object of the ritual is *not* the particular concrete means used. Then small deviations in procedure are not a problem so long as sacredness is maintained.

PROBLEMS WITH UNDERSTANDING RELIGIOUS LANGUAGE

Concretism. Religious language necessarily uses concrete images and symbols to stand for abstract notions. When people understand these concretely, they live in a very shrunken and narrow world.

They cannot stand changes in the way belief statements are worded, in the order or symbols of ritual, or in interpretations of religious propositions. Changes rock their entire belief structure. They become disturbed — even to the point of panic — when any change occurs in religious imagery, ritual, or symbols.

Concrete thinkers cannot adequately deal with religious symbolism because they do not understand analogy and metaphor. When analogies are used, concrete thinkers see only the similarity between the terms, and not the differences. When such people hear God called "father," they are trapped into understanding God only in terms of their personal experience with fathers. They cannot see that "father" refers to qualities like caring guidance, tender love, being made of the same "stuff," or provision of needs.

Concrete thinkers feel threatened when someone who finds other connotations of "father" too troublesome to ignore refers to God with a different word to express these same qualities — such as "mother," "wisdom," or "teacher." When a women's religious conference celebrated God as Sophia, the Hebrew Bible's Eternal Wisdom, one outraged theologian screamed, "They are trying to take God's fatherhood away from him! They can't arbitrarily decide what God is like!"[11]

To the concrete mind, any change in the traditional ways can be truly earth-shattering. Such occasions might draw quite extreme reactions. The threat involved in such changes may "produce irrational fantasies of persecution, revenge, and world catastrophe."[12] Some concrete thinkers believe that an insidious plot is behind every proposed change in religious procedures.

Literalism. A near cousin to concretism is literalism. Literal interpretation considers only "the letter," the obvious surface meaning of the words, rather than any deeper significance. It emphasizes what the words denote rather than their connotations. Some religions encourage "radically literal interpretation of scriptures, which refuse to admit any change whatsoever. [This] shows an inability to come to grips with mere possibilities, assumptions, or speculations. The world has shrunk to visible and tangible realities."[13] Christian mystic St. John of the Cross considered taking things at face value, understanding too literally, a major difficulty in the spiritual life. Literalism does not penetrate spiritual meaning, but rests in facile superficiality. "Souls are misled by understanding according to the letter, the outer rind. Anyone bound to the letter cannot avoid serious error and will later become confused for not having made room for the spirit stripped of the letter. The soul should renounce the literal sense, for faith is incomprehensible to the senses."[14]

I once met a clergyman whose denomination I had heard was quite literal and fundamental and asked him about his tradition. He said that people accuse it of being excessively literal, but that his people know when religious language is not literal. He explained that when the Old Testament says that all flesh is grass, that does not mean that our bodies are made of grass. On the other hand, he emphasized, when it says that God created the world in seven days, that's different. I politely thanked him and said I understood.

RELIGIOUS LANGUAGE AND
THE SEARCH FOR FAITH

Cautions. As religious movements become large, the founder's message becomes more codified. Many religious people then read symbolic religious language concretely.[15] They overlook subtleties and read the prophet's metaphors as if literally true. "Heaven" becomes some physical place rather than a state of being. "God" might become a ruler on a throne in the sky. Relinquishing such encrustation is constantly necessary but must be done carefully. Sri Aurobindo cautioned, "In its endeavor to get rid of the superstition and ignorance [in] religious forms and symbols, intellectual reason unenlightened by spiritual knowledge tends to deny and destroy the truth contained in them."[16]

For a symbol to be "true" it must evoke in us what it is meant to evoke; this is different from conceptual, logical, historical, or scientific truth. Once a religious organization has cast its message into dogmas and creeds, however, it often does not allow members to use alternative symbols to express religious meaning. People differ in their ability to see past such restrictions; for some it causes serious faith problems. They "may, on the basis of a literal, naive, unexamined interpretation of religion, reject all religion." Other people remain able to use "religious statements to seek their deeper symbolic meanings which lie beyond their literal wording."[17]

For growth. To grow spiritually, we must let symbols speak to us and refuse to translate them literally or in some preconceived fashion. Sri Aurobindo said that we must "abandon a too persistent attachment to forms of faith and cling to the saving reality alone."[18] We do not want to clutch the rind and throw away the sweet fruit that it covers. Concrete, literal, unilateral interpretations of religious statements do just that.

We must have faith in the stories "not in the sense of believing them so much as taking them seriously. To believe in a tale of the gods may be no more than gullibility or intellectual error. To have faith in a myth, on the other hand, is to take it to heart, to recognize its human implications and to accept them as implicating oneself."[19]

Chapter 4

FAITH'S PLACES OF REFUGE

TEACHER, TEACHINGS, AND COMMUNITY

I [do not] believe in the Church as an authoritarian institution
with all the answers; it has never been very believable in that
guise anyway, nor, for that matter true to itself.

— EUGENE KENNEDY[1]

What is the object or refuge of faith? This varies from person to
person, but we can define several major arenas. The Buddha spoke of
faith in one's teacher, the teachings themselves, and the community
built on the teachings.[2] In these the spiritual seeker takes refuge.
This chapter studies each of these objects of faith, which all point to
the Ultimate Reality itself, across faith traditions.

THE TEACHER

In the various traditions around the world, people understand their
chief religious figure very similarly. They commonly hold their high
teachers to embody the Godhead in a very special way, seeing them
as incarnations or *avatars*[3] of God. Christians tend to accept just
one *avatar*, Jesus, while other traditions usually admit various *avatars*.
They would argue that different cultures, times, and circumstances
call for hearing from God in a variety of ways.

Jesus and the Word. Some theologians have suggested that the
Christ should not be equated with the man Jesus,[4] "is not to be confused with the historic Jesus."[5] The Christ is the Eternal Word of

God. The Word's manifestation in history is not necessarily limited to Jesus. While Jesus *is* the Word incarnate, he does not "use up" the Word. The Word of God *could* appear in other incarnations or guises. The Word of God — not the human person Jesus — mediates salvation in whatever way or form the Word "chooses."

Jesus himself defined his role as being sent to the "lost children of Israel" (Matthew 15:24); that he later became a more universal figure does not negate this statement. He also, clearly speaking as God incarnate and not just the man Jesus, said that he had other sheep not of this flock to which he must tend (John 10:16). He did not tell his Jewish disciples to run out and make these other people members of their fold but said that he himself must tend them.

Understanding avatars. Sri Aurobindo explained that *avatars* manifest the divine nature in human nature so that we can mold our being on the lines of that Christhood, Krishnahood, or Buddhahood. "The Christ, Krishna, Buddha, makes through himself the way [we] must follow. That is why each Incarnation holds before [us] his own example and declares of himself that he is the way and the gate; he declares too the oneness of his humanity with the Divine being."[6]

Avatars all make the same claims. In the *Bhagavad-Gita*, Krishna said, "Whenever there is decline of virtue and the rise of evil, I send myself forth. For the deliverance of the good, for the destruction of evil, I am born from age to age."[7] Buddhists hold that Buddhas manifest at appropriate times. A Mahayana Buddhist scripture teaches, "The exalted one appears in the world for salvation to many people, for joy to many people, out of compassion for the world, as a blessing, as a salvation, as the joy of gods and humans."[8]

Krishna identified himself in the *Gita* as the highest Godhead. "I am the origin, dissolution, and maintenance of apparent existence, the imperishable seed of all existences and their eternal resting place."[9] Gotama, the Buddha, said of himself, "One who sees *Dhamma* sees me; one who sees me, sees *Dhamma*. Seeing *Dhamma*, one also sees me. Seeing me, one sees *Dhamma*."[10] The Buddha's identification with the *Dhamma* parallels that of Jesus with the *Logos*, the Word of God.[11] The Buddha's statement is like Jesus' saying, "One who has seen me has seen the Father. Believe me that I am in the Father, and the Father in me" (John 14:9, 11) or "I am the Way, the Truth, and the Life" (John 14:6).

The lives imputed to these religious figures are also highly similar. They have in common such elements as miraculous conception and visitation by wise people who "recognized" the child and predicted future spiritual greatness. Their great compassionate love produced miraculous healing and other miracles. Many were transfigured into glory and had psychic powers. Humans tend to create similar mythologies about their *avatars*. Their traditions present all these figures in ways that make them suitable objects of devotion, which can greatly support the life of faith. For a person of grounded faith, committed to a spiritual path, these similarities need be no problem.

THE TEACHINGS

Scholars widely acknowledge that many teachings in all these traditions reflect more a consensus of the early community than the specific instruction of one teacher. Scholars trying to determine the authentic words of Jesus consider their work difficult and say that it often challenges their own faith. One said, "My interest in encountering Jesus is not to confirm my own prejudices, but to be delivered from a stunted soul."[12] Another leading scholar of the origins of gospel teachings said, "Modern scholarship enables us to hear the different voices in the gospels, and that makes them much richer."[13]

The Egyptian teachings attributed to Hermes Trismegistus are an interesting counterpoint to the teachings of Jesus, Gotama, and Krishna. Once considered inspired by the god Hermes, scholars now agree that these teachings had multiple authors. All were written within a fairly narrow time band, most likely several hundred years after the time of Christ. They are as coherent a body of teachings as those attributed to the Buddha or the Christ. Since no formal organizational structure developed to promote these teachings as the work of one divine source, no mythology of an incarnate divine teacher was formulated. The teachings stand by themselves as the thought of a small, like-minded group of thinkers who read and built upon a few core mystical understandings.[14]

The outer teachings of all traditions are deeply embedded in the cultures in which they arose. Hence, they show obvious differences. The mystical teachings — teachings leading to intuitive, unmediated loving-knowledge of God — are very similar in all traditions. Because we Westerners tend to think "substantively," while the East thinks "relationally," we often find recognizing these similarities difficult. "The substance paradigm stresses permanence, being and separateness; and, the relational paradigm stresses transiency, becoming, and relatedness."[15] Some Western mystics think somewhat like Easterners, so reading them makes it easier to grasp how similar these teachings are.

THE COMMUNITY

Religious communities start in various ways. The Hindu community existed before specific devotion to the *avatar* Krishna. With the Buddha and the Christ, communities developed around teachings attributed to a historical figure. The communities of religious traditions have major differences in their structure and activities. Deeply embedded in its own culture and also shaped by various individuals with personal agendas, each community reflects unique needs and biases. Beneath these surface differences, the best in all of them adheres to similar important conclusions about community.

Ironical twists. Today's institutionalized religious organizations would probably astonish their founding teachers; they would also astonish the earliest communities. The Christian church now is often a bureaucratic, top-heavy, authoritarian structure very similar to what Jesus railed against in the Gospel of Matthew (chap. 23). Read how he addressed the Pharisees about their religious structures to see if it does not sound disturbingly familiar.

The egalitarian society that the Buddha envisioned is often negated by the special consideration given ordained monks. The Buddha wanted no castes based on position, but only "castes" based on meritorious behavior. Yet, in Buddhist cultures, monks — regardless of their virtue or lack of it — are clearly a caste above all other people. The Buddha's wish that they never burden other people has yielded to societies that give monks the best of everything, even when others go without basic necessities to do so.

Sri Aurobindo explained such problems. He said that society mechanizes religion, binding it to socio-religious trappings that impose "an imperious yoke and an iron prison." It sets up churches, priesthoods, and ceremonies. Like watchdogs they defend their creeds and dogmas, dogmas that "one had to accept and obey under pain of condemnation to eternal hell. This false socialization of religion has been always the chief cause of its failure to regenerate [humanity]."[16]

The foundational rock. When Jesus asked Peter who he thought he (Jesus) was, Peter inspiredly blurted out that he was the Messiah. Jesus was properly impressed, recognizing Peter's deep spiritual insight. He celebrated this, saying that no human reasoning or understanding produced that answer. Jesus then told Peter that he was "really solid stuff," and that he (Jesus) would gather his people on this solid stuff (Matthew 16:15–18).

Clearly the "solid stuff" was Peter's capacity for spiritual insight leading to faith, not his person, his strength of character, or his leadership ability. When "the chips were down," Peter ran. When he and Paul later fought over management of the early church, Paul won.[17] When Peter fell back into worldly thinking and failed to demonstrate this "solid stuff," Jesus strongly scolded him, calling him Satan (Matthew 16:21–23) — peculiar behavior had Peter just been put in charge of all of Jesus' people.

Yet, interestingly, the Catholic Church, inspired by Roman legal thinking, presents this passage as meaning that Jesus gave Peter dogmatic primacy over other followers. Needless to point out, other Christians — Protestants and Eastern Orthodox — do not agree with this conclusion. Nor do all Catholics, as both our opening quote and the following one suggest. "You know the Church suffers from overadministration. Maybe once in a while, instead of seeming to say the last word on a subject, we could just say that we really don't understand."[18]

Bonding and forgiveness. What kind of community was Jesus trying to gather? He gave Peter the key to understanding this community, the key to the kingdom that he said was within us (Luke

17:21). The community was to be one of mutual forgiveness — because only when we can find it within our hearts to forgive another, *truly* forgive, is the divisiveness of hurting behavior healed. If we hold on to another's "sin" against us, nothing — not even heaven — can heal the damage (Matthew 16:19).

Jesus considered it very important that his followers understand this. Shortly thereafter (Matthew 17:18) he repeated this "key to the kingdom" to a larger group of followers. To be sure they got the point, Jesus embedded the teaching in stories of forgiveness and failing to forgive. When later, at the Last Supper, he prayed that all be one with each other, him, and God (John 17:21), the point of all this becomes even more evident. If we cannot establish solidarity and bonded caring among ourselves, how can we hope to have it with God, with our Source and the Source of all others?

Psychologist Hobart Mowrer argued that Alcoholics Anonymous is the nearest contemporary approximation to the earliest Christian community. Here people openly acknowledge failures, confess them, and actively work to repair any harm done. Those following Twelve Step spirituality commit themselves to an examined life, admit mistakes and their need for help, and help others as they have been helped. According to Mowrer, such a program closely captures the spirit of early Christianity.[19]

A lamp unto oneself. The Buddha's last teaching was that his followers were to become lamps unto themselves.[20] They were to look within, within that "fathom-long body" in which the Buddha said all is to be found.[21] Both Jesus and the Buddha thus agreed that we find "the kingdom" within.

The Buddha's instructions on the community of mutual support and assistance were the same as those of Jesus. He told his monks that taking care of each other was taking care of him: "whoever, monks, would tend me, should tend the sick."[22] Jesus reflected this sentiment when he said, "To the extent you gave to others, even the least of them, you did it to me. To the extent that you did not give to one of the least of these, you did not do it to me" (Matthew 25:40, 45).

The Buddha's community, like that of Jesus, was not to have positions of dictatorship, but was to gather for mutual support and service. Before putting faith in any tradition, we would do well to consider the understanding of community that the early faith gathering held. It will be this service model, which seems to be a basic universal religious position. Putting faith in structures that have evolved over time according to the dictates of expediency, political maneuvering, and various other motives is not trusting the best understanding of community.

THE ULTIMATE REALITY

Ultimately, none of these refuges of faith validly exists solely in its own right; all must point toward the Ultimate Reality, toward loving knowledge of God. Sri Aurobindo noted that the deepest heart of religion stands apart from the outward machinery of creed, cult, ceremony, and symbol. It is the search for and finding of God. "Its aspiration is to discover the Infinite, the Absolute, the One, the Divine. Its work is a sincere, absolute surrender and service, a casting of every part of our existence out of its normal status into an uprush towards the Divine."[23]

SUMMARY

We can value devotion toward the spiritual founder, appreciate the consensus of faith derived from the viewpoints of the early community, and recognize what in community helps us grow toward God and what does not. We can use what is good and appropriate in these objects of faith, while we discard what is not. We must proceed carefully so that we do not prematurely discard what is helping us and do not cling beyond its usefulness to what is not. This requires great discernment. Keeping the final goal in mind is our guide and protection.

Part II

PROBLEMS IN UNDERSTANDING FAITH

Chapter 5

FAITH IS NOT WHAT YOU BELIEVE

FREEDOM FROM OPINIONS

Faith is not belief, and with the partial exception of a brief aberrant moment in recent Church history, no serious and careful religious thinker has ever held that it was.

— WILFRED CANTWELL SMITH[1]

Faith is *not* what we believe.[2] That is, faith is not conceptual conclusions or opinions; faith also is not the beliefs we formulate to express our faith. Treating faith as such creates unnecessary divisions among people. It goes contrary to the great mystics' teachings. Also, "believing is not what in those [early] centuries Baptism and the Creeds were about."[3] Abhishiktananda wrote, "Faith does not consist in acceptance of certain propositions, termed 'data of revelation.' The various 'revelations' enshrined in the different religions are simply the reports [of people] whose inward gaze has pierced as far as those depths."[4]

People in all traditions try to formulate their faith conceptually, and this produces belief systems. In the West, belief systems are often imposed upon people either as *being* their faith or as forming its basis. Many people hold such religious beliefs as rigid opinions that lack an experiential basis.

Considering beliefs a basis for faith is utterly foreign to Eastern spiritual thought. The Buddha said not to believe anything that any-

one tells you, no matter on what authority — and that included what
he himself said.[5] The saying, "If you meet the Buddha on the road,
kill him," means not to give "lip service" to teachings on outer authority. We verify in our own experience what we adopt so that it is
no longer mere belief. Eastern traditions agree that we should never
affirm what we have not tested and that we should reserve judgment
about all untried teachings.

Two distinct words in the Muslim *Qur'an*[6] are often both translated as belief. One means to have faith, the other to hold an
opinion.[7] "Between what is designated by conjuring up fond fancies
and responding positively to God's clear summons (faith), the con-
trast is stark. The divergence here between belief in this sense and
faith in true sense is the difference between Hell and Heaven."[8]

BUDDHIST TEACHINGS ON THE BASES
FOR HOLDING OPINIONS

In Buddhist teachings, faith has little to do with opinions, ideas, or
beliefs. Faith is one of five factors on which we base conceptual notions, which may or may not be factual. These bases for opinions
are: faith, preference, tradition, arguing upon evidence, and liking
to ponder on views.[9] Since the West frequently equates beliefs with
faith, let us carefully study these bases.

Faith. Buddhists say faith develops from experience. They do not
a priori believe things to be true; they *find* them to be true in their
spiritual practice. Faith may then lead to beliefs based on that experience and also to opinions that range beyond it. Faith is only one
of five possible bases for beliefs and is not equated with either mere
opinions or experience-based beliefs.

Preference. Simply put, preference means we believe what we
want to believe, hold the opinions we like. This is true for religious
ideas as well as others. Such wish-based opinions are the content of
some people's faith. If you ask each person in a crowded religious
assembly what God is, you get a variety of answers. For the lonely,
God is a friend; for the fearful, God is a protecting caretaker; for one
needing guidance, God is a parent — and so forth.

Sri Aurobindo understood these mental proclivities. "Spiritual philosophy convinces the rational mind only where the intellect is already predisposed to belief, and even if it convinces, it cannot give the true knowledge. It is apt to harden into an intellectual system and to present the form as if it were the essence."[10]

Psychologist Freud held that people adopt religious beliefs because of unresolved dependency needs; they want the security of feeling that someone is taking care of them. He said such beliefs exert strong control over people because they are "fulfillments of the oldest, strongest and most urgent wishes of [human beings]. The secret of their strength lies in the strength of these wishes."[11]

Freud was undoubtedly right about some people. We *do* create God in the images to which our needs draw us, and we take these images to be God. Such "faith" is basically insecure, because at some level we realize it is based primarily on desire or fear. When threatened with disconfirming information, such believers may fight very hard for their images of God, trying to bolster uncertain beliefs.

This is one reason why the Buddha did not use God-concepts, although his teachings do include ideas that correspond to God-understandings in other faiths. Many Christian mystics also urge us to let go of all concepts, ideas, and images of God. Worshiping understandings of God created by desire is idolatry. Idolatry leaves no room to find the true Ultimate Reality.

Tradition. Tradition is a very common basis for beliefs. Remember that the Buddha said not to believe anything simply because you were told it, no matter how positively you feel about the authority speaking.[12] Initially this advice seems quite counter to Christian teachings, but let us understand what the Buddha meant before rejecting it. He encouraged people to try out religious teachings and to discover their fruits. Practical living then either confirms or disconfirms a teaching's value. The Christian heritage holds similar notions: to taste the Lord, to know the value of something by its fruits (Psalm 34:8; Matthew 7:16, 20).

Like the Buddha, Jesus also taught that mere belief is not proper faith. He said those who simply cry out, "Lord, Lord" are not doing enough (Luke 6:46–49). The apostle James said, "The demons also believe and shudder" (James 2:19). Jesus also very harshly condemned those who bind others unthinkingly to tradition; the Gospel

of Matthew is rich in such passages.[13] Any time we retreat into
merely mouthing words, we are going for a "cheap grace" that neither Jesus nor the Buddha would support. Vedanta also advises:
"Do not depend on doctrines. Show by your lives that religion does
not mean words, or names, or sects, but that it means spiritual
realization."[14]

Evidence. Arguing on the bases of evidence is the way of scholars.
Psychologist William James wrote disparagingly about theological
debate. He held that all the mental manipulations of scholars are
"secondary accretions" to the heart of religion, which is experience.[15] Sri Aurobindo agreed: "Even the highest philosophizing
cannot give a true inner knowledge, is not the spiritual light, does
not open the gates of experience."[16] Yet, "a great many Christian
theologians make an effort to prove that religious faith itself is a 'rational act,' [though] nobody ever arrived at faith from a process of
reasoning."[17]

Buddhists argue that concepts have no basic, enduring reality.
Any conclusions they reach are flimsy at best, since the premises of
all argumentation are human mental creations. Sri Aurobindo wrote,
"Logic is the worst enemy of Truth, as self-righteousness is the worst
enemy of virtue; for the one cannot see its own errors nor the other
its own imperfections."[18] Another way to put this is to realize that
any idea *about* God is *not* God — a point St. John of the Cross
repeatedly emphasizes.[19]

Proofs for the existence of God, or for the validity of any theological opinion, are only words. "The knowledge of God is not gained
by weighing the feeble arguments of reason for or against [God's]
existence; it is gained only by a self-transcending and absolute conse-
cration, aspiration and experience. Nor does that experience proceed
by anything like rational scientific experiment or rational philosophic
thinking."[20]

Pondering. The less scholarly activity of pondering notions is just
enjoying our own thinking processes. We let conclusions arise from
the wanderings of the mind on opinions we hear or create. Such
pondering often follows genuine spiritual intuition, but spoils it by
adding our own mental activity. This almost certainly distorts the
insight.

St. John of the Cross said that, when God gives a grace, everything needed is there in the giving. We do not improve it by adding our own analysis.[21] Buddhists argue that only direct experience, which *does* include intuitive knowledge, puts us in touch with reality. Only this understanding rests on solid ground. Both agree on the uselessness of philosophizing. It most often leads us into unfounded opinions to which we then tightly cling.

Summary. The Buddha summarized his teachings on such bases for opinions: "Do not make the basis for belief an authoritative tradition, an unbroken succession, conformity with scriptures, metaphysical theories, inference, rational reflection, agreement with opinions you already hold, competence of any person, or respect for what a teacher thinks. Abandon what you know for yourself leads to ill and accept what leads to good."[22]

TEACHINGS ON DEALING WITH BELIEFS

The insistence of opinions. Philosopher Alan Watts contrasted faith and belief to show the error of considering beliefs to be religious faith. He said that belief sits down in the middle of the road to suck the thumb pointing to the truth, instead of following to where it points. Believers insist that reality be structured as they say it is, while faith is openness to truth, however it may be. "Belief clings, but faith lets go."[23]

Beliefs at best interpret our own religious experiences, not itself a helpful activity. Often they come from someone else's intellectual pondering, given us as a faith object. Beliefs tend to impose immutability on experience and can lead to tunnel-vision definitions of what cannot be captured in concepts. Beliefs frequently obscure what is essential. Watts said that the more beliefs we have — the more we insist on the truth value of particular interpretations — the less room we have for the openness that faith demands.

Sri Aurobindo said that truth is hidden from rationalists because they are convinced that their own reason is right and the reason of others who differ is wrong. Rationalists also underestimate the deficiencies of the human intellect and consider it able to found human thought and life securely on a clear, rational basis. These stances are "no doubt the common expression of our egoism and arrogant fallibility."[24]

The inadequacy of formulas. Such notions agree well with those of highly acclaimed mystics. Like others of his times, St. John of the Cross used Christian terms to formulate his faith; this was the only religious tradition's terminology that he knew. But he saw words for the inadequate instruments they are and said that we must let go of all concepts, memories, ideas, images, to come to deeper understanding of God.[25] We must let go of all words and beliefs that are objects of idolatry, that are themselves taken to be the Holy. We must relinquish all formulas that make our life of faith rigid.

St. John's words on this: "Persons are decidedly hindered from union with God when they are attached to any understanding, feeling, imagining, opinion, desire, or way of their own. Their goal transcends all this, even the loftiest object that can be known or experienced."[26] John's point is that any thoughts or images of God are *not* God. This holds true whether they are notions of God to which we come personally or ones we accept on another person's word. The formula is *not* God.

Faith is not the words, concepts, thoughts, ideas, or images with which we try to communicate our faith and which many people take to be the objects of faith. John also claims that all this conceptual activity cannot bring us to God. He explicitly so warns people who believe that thinking a lot about God is a good idea.[27] We come to God only by "setting our hearts on God's being."[28]

The confusion of faith and belief. The relation between faith and belief, as Thomas Aquinas saw them, "has been obscured, not to say obfuscated, by a tendency to translate his word for the initiatory 'act of faith,' *credo,* by the verb 'believe.'"[29] Scholar W. C. Smith said that Thomas held faith to be a relation to truth as such, not to opinion, and only incidentally to any particular formulation of truth or set of beliefs. "The role of explicit belief in his articulated view of faith is minor and even at times negative."[30]

Panikkar also distinguished between faith and beliefs. Faith, our inner relation to what is beyond us, has its own light that can never fade. Beliefs are the symbols through which faith tries to be manifest at the mental level.[31] Thomas Aquinas stated that some people of sound faith hold erroneous beliefs, which are determined by their historical situation. All formulations of faith, all beliefs, are human, while faith itself remains divine.[32]

Confusing the symbol for the object of faith is a serious error. It binds us to one formulation of faith alone. We fail to see how spiritual seekers across traditions are bonded in a more broadly defined faith.

A contemporary Buddhist teaching. Martin Luther King nominated Buddhist monk Thich Nhat Hanh for the Nobel Peace Prize in 1967. The first three precepts taken by members of Nhat Hanh's spiritual order reflect the Buddhist horror of clinging to opinions and offer deep wisdom.

First: "Do not be idolatrous about or bound to any doctrine, theory, or ideology, even Buddhist ones. All systems of thought are guiding means; they are not absolute truth."

Second: "Do not think the knowledge you presently possess is changeless, absolute truth. Avoid being narrow-minded and bound to present views. Learn and practice non-attachment from views in order to be open to receive others' viewpoints. Truth is found in life and not merely in conceptual knowledge. Be ready to learn throughout your entire life and to observe reality in yourself and in the world at all times."

Third: "Do not force others, including children, by any means whatsoever, to adopt your views, whether by authority, threat, money, propaganda, or even education. However, through compassionate dialogue, help others renounce fanaticism and narrowness."[33]

CONCLUSIONS

For the Muslim, " 'infidelity,' the heinous sin, the incomprehensibly stupid and perverse obduracy, is not unbelief but 'refusal'; it is a spitting in God's face when [God] speaks out of infinite authority and vast compassion."[34] We would do well to understand this distinction. So often we consider agreeing with certain doctrinal or creedal statements to be the essence of faith.

The contemporary church seems to say that "believing is the price that one must pay, in order to have faith."[35] Because we usually articulate faith in terms of earlier beliefs of the spiritual community, abandoning beliefs feels like abandoning faith. Yet "it might be faith itself that would impel some to differ. Theology [has] become the almost amoral prior condition of being allowed to have [faith]."[36]

Chapter 6

FAITH IS NOT FEELING SURE

THE PROBLEM OF RELIGIOUS CERTAINTY

Faith [cannot] be either increased or diminished by acquiring rational certitude or losing it.

— ETIENNE GILSON[1]

Most people want to feel certain about something before investing themselves in it. They often then cling to certainty in growth-stunting ways. Yet, "it is a characteristic of the mature mind that it can act wholeheartedly even without absolute certainty."[2] This chapter explores religious certainty and discusses it in relation to mental and spiritual health.

THE PULL TO CERTAINTY

Religious certainty usually refers to religious beliefs and opinions. Why do some people cling so tightly to beliefs while others can be more open-minded? We find several possible reasons.

The pressure for orthodoxy. Many people are taught that right faith means holding correct ideas with a convinced certainty. The more sophisticated of them acknowledge the role of honest and helpful doubt about religious ideas. Yet they may still insist that we must ultimately consider our own tradition's formulations to be the most complete, the final word of God, or the perfect truth.

We are also told we must word our understanding in official creeds or in church-approved language. The ferocity with which we defend and promulgate creedal positions reveals a spirit difficult to reconcile with living faith in God or goodness. We make ourselves unable to appreciate others' experiences, concepts, symbols, or moral conclusions. "If we adopt definite views, we get concerned about defending them. This leads to disputations with rival doctrines, resulting in pride. The true seer has shaken off all views having no view to defend, no prejudice to plead."[3]

Security blankets. When people need unshakable beliefs to feel secure, they cannot tolerate any threat to their certainty. Such use of religious understandings seriously stultifies personal growth.[4] Jesus did not endorse such "faith." When the Pharisees informed him that surely they were not blind, Jesus replied: "Blind? If you were, you would not be guilty, but since you say, 'We see,' your guilt remains" (John 9:41).

St. John of the Cross explained this passage: "Those who both live in darkness and blind themselves to all their natural lights will have supernatural vision, and those who want to lean on some light of their own will become blind and be held back on this road leading to union."[5] How many people lean on the "light" of words and ideas about God — either their own or those handed them by others — instead of seeking union with God!

For their own security reasons, religious institutions often encourage people to cling to particular formulations. "True believers," who simply swallow without question what leaders tell them, make running an organization easier. How many churches do exactly what Jesus condemned in the Pharisees! A teaching from Vedanta is instructive. "Into blind darkness enter those who worship ignorance. Those who delight in their knowledge go into even greater darkness."[6]

DOGMATISM

Dogmatic certainty. Psychologist William James rather humorously wrote that dogmatic people *know* that what *they* know is true *is* true. "There is indeed nothing which someone has not thought absolutely true, while [a] neighbor deemed it absolutely false; and not an absolutist among them seems ever to have considered that the intellect, even when truth is directly in its grasp, may have no infallible signal for knowing whether it be truth or no."[7]

Accepting the word of an "infallible" source is just one other belief that we have no infallible way to evaluate! The new Catholic catechism states that faith is certain because it is founded on the word of God who cannot lie.[8] This seems to beg the question that the very notion of where and how one arrives at the word of God is itself another article of faith.

We laugh at the pronouncement of Parson Thwackum in Henry Fielding's *Tom Jones:* "When I mention religion, I mean the Christian religion, and not only the Christian religion, but the Protestant religion, and not only the Protestant religion, but the Church of England."[9] Yet many people have similar notions like, "*Of course,* my religious opinions are absolute truth. It's too bad that others are misguided, or in error or bad faith, but that doesn't change the truth of my understanding."

Abhishiktananda says that religious people are naturally tempted to attribute absolute value to their own conceptual formulas and their tradition's structures. He warns us, though, that these forms are only continually changing attempts to express "a reality which is essentially beyond all expression. These expressions are also essentially limited by the particular conditions of the period, language and culture of the milieu in which they come to birth."[10]

Understanding dogmatism. Dogmatism insists that things be as one says they are. Immature people react dogmatically when they feel their certainty about what they believe is being threatened.[11] "The religion of maturity makes the affirmation 'God is,' but only the religion of immaturity will insist 'God is precisely what I say.' "[12]

"To be in possession of an absolute truth is to have a net of familiarity spread over the whole of eternity. There are no surprises and no unknowns. All questions have already been answered, all decisions made, all eventualities foreseen. The true believer is without wonder and hesitation."[13] Eric Hoffer held that such credulity is often joined with a proneness to lying. "The inability or unwillingness to see things as they are promotes both gullibility and charlatanism."[14]

Religious institutions also become dogmatic when they are threat-

ened. Religions commonly begin with a prophetic figure who attracts
a following. When the following gets sufficiently large, the fearful existing orthodoxy labels it a heresy and persecutes it. If the movement
survives persecution, it becomes a new orthodoxy. Its followers then
stone new prophets who threaten them. This cycle repeats itself over
and over again in history.[15]

Those who need simplistic understandings to feel safe or comfortable in life are easily victimized by dogmatic movements. We need
to discern the difference between using religious beliefs as a security blanket and appropriate surrender to that which is greater than
us. Unresolved dependency needs can bend us toward manipulating
God or our own minds to fill our wishes[16] — a stance the opposite
of truly surrendered faith.

THE UNHEALTHINESS OF CERTAINTY

Paranoid thought. Paranoid thought illustrates extreme need for
certainty. No one is more certain that their opinions are true than
paranoid persons, and paranoia is the most incurable psychiatric syn-
drome. Paranoids' logic is flawless once we accept their premises,
so they cannot be argued out of non-factual opinions. Their flawed
premises are untouchable givens. These beliefs are so grounded in
personal need that relinquishing them would psychologically feel like
death. "The madman is not the man who has lost his reason. The
madman is the man who has lost everything except his reason."[17]

Paranoids highlight an uncomfortable fact: the strength with
which one holds convictions bears absolutely no relationship to their
truth value. How strongly we believe something says nothing about
how factual that belief is. For religious beliefs, the strength of cognitive conviction usually depends on how intensely we were socialized
into the formulations of our tradition and how strongly we need
certainty.

Idolatry. People can become idolatrous without ever realizing it.
One psychologist of religion defined the essence of idolatry as "the
deification of things, of partial aspects of the world."[18] Every time we
treat a symbol or particular religious means as if it were the Ultimate
Reality, we engage in idolatry. "Those who adopt a particular form

and have not reached the formless truth are inclined to regard their relative truth as absolute and confuse eternal truths with historic facts."[19]

Psychologist David Bakan said that idolatry is too quickly fixing on some single method or notion as the ultimate fulfillment of religion. The idolatrous mind allows particular religious objects to be ultimate. "The history of the Judeo-Christian religion is filled with instances in which a means of fulfilling the religious impulse became the object of worship itself."[20] Ritual, scripture, religious art — any religious act or artifact — can become an object of idolatry.[21]

Many Muslims mean by "There is no God but Allah" that any non-Muslim understanding of God is erroneous. However, one Sufi Muslim position holds that this affirmation simply tells us to avoid idolatry.[22] We are not to worship passing, temporal things, but only that which is Ultimate. This stance encourages us to recognize any idolatry in how we use religious means. So often we turn scripture or belief statements into objects of idolatry; we take them to be the Holy itself. We get trapped in dogmas, creeds, and other conceptualizations. We have erected many "graven images" in our formulations.

Clinging to something past its usefulness is also idolatry. The Buddha said that teachings are like a raft used to cross a river; once across, we do not continue to carry it with us.[23] We must know when to hold on to and when to release particular means. A Vedantic Upanishad rather drastically urges, "Read, study and ceaselessly ponder the Scriptures; but once the light has shined within you, throw them away as you discard a brand which you have used to light your fire."[24]

THE IMPORTANCE OF HONESTY

Reflect on the great religious teachers. They all condemned the entrenched religious establishment of their own times for close-mindedly foisting its own positions on others. Both the Christ and the Buddha clearly did so. Yet their followers created religious bureaucracies that indulge in the exact behavior they condemned. We can save ourselves from this trap by remembering that authority claimed for any beliefs not based on our own direct seeing is simply another opinion.

Recognizing the pull to comfort. Clinging to conceptual notions can be extremely comforting. Fixed beliefs feel firm, stable, and unchanging. Experience changes, but concepts last. We can become addicted to the comfort of concepts, of our inflexible opinions. They leave us feeling that everything is under control, that all is secure. But faith is not a matter of felt certainty.

Our mental activity is always necessarily mixed with some amount of error. We should not allow our faith to be upset when we discover our errors. "The human intellect is too much afraid of error precisely because it is too much attached to a premature sense of certitude and a too hasty eagerness for positive finality in what it seems to seize of knowledge."[25]

Releasing certainty. For broader understanding, we must rupture established security. We must realize that our own religious ideas are not necessarily superior to others and admit that other people reach toward the good and the true as we do ourselves. This means seeing ourselves and our own religious tradition as seekers among other seekers rather than as truth-possessors in the midst of ignorant, arrogant, erroneous, or poor-faithed others.

Near the end of Jesus' encounter with the Samaritan woman at the well, he said that her people do not understand what they are doing in worship, but that the Jews know what they worship. This is often interpreted as endorsing the Jewish understanding. But look at what Jesus says next! He discards both of those stances, saying that the time is coming when "true worshippers will worship the Father in spirit and truth" (John 4:21–24). So much for certainty about what one is doing!

Psychologist Gordon Allport said, "An heuristic belief is one that is held tentatively until it can be confirmed or until it helps us discover a more valid belief."[26] He considered this way essential for mature faith. Sometimes we must relinquish particular beliefs or how we formulate a belief. How can people hold beliefs loosely, with willingness to revise them as needed, and yet act wholeheartedly in religious endeavor? It seems to depend on the role of faith in a person's life. When thirst for God is strong enough, we let go of what we must relinquish and understand "the wisdom of insecurity."[27]

A traumatic awakening. A prominent psychologist of religion said, "Faith is [a] working hypothesis...a risk."[28] How liberating such understanding is! The comfort of certainty is just *not* what faith means. When I consulted priests about faith as a young woman, I expected faith to feel certain and I was far from certain. I wanted the cause to be something wrong with me so that it could be fixed and I could have the security of certainty.

One priest finally told me I was wrong, that faith is wanting God so badly you spend your entire life seeking God. Because I had strongly believed that faith *had* to be certain, disconfirmation of this opinion devastated me. I was absolutely terrified. That evening I drove far out into the country, well over the speed limit, and sat in my car most of the night arguing with God. "It isn't fair that I'm supposed to base my entire life on something and can't even feel sure that it's true!" Anger eventually turned to fear, then pleading, then resignation, and finally a spark of surrender.

A final comment. What, then, can we honestly say about certainty and faith? We must accept the hard fact that subjective certainty about any particular tradition or any given belief is not a sign of its truth. Similarly, doubt is not a sign that it lacks truth. The final word goes to Alan Watts: "If you try to capture running water in a bucket, it is clear that you do not understand it and that you will always be disappointed, for in the bucket the water does not run. To 'have' running water you must let go of it and let it run. The same is true of life and of God."[29]

Chapter 7

FAITH IS NOT BLIND

THE NEED FOR HARD QUESTIONS

What we know as blind faith is sustained by innumerable un-
beliefs. The true believer [has] ability to "shut his eyes and stop
his ears" to facts.

— ERIC HOFFER[1]

Strong forces encourage blind faith. Early religious education for
many people is unfortunately only simple indoctrination. Few traditions are free of this difficulty. If we are to come to spiritual
adulthood, at some time in our lives we must examine what others
have taught us.

Recognizing blindness in our faith is not always easy. We take many
unquestioned assumptions for granted, not ever realizing that they are
matters of opinion. When we rest in our assumptions without examining them, we are in blind faith — which is really not faith at all.

THE CASE AGAINST BLIND FAITH

The Christ. Some people read Jesus' statement to the apostle
Thomas, extolling those who have not seen but have believed (John
20:29), as encouraging us to accept blindly whatever we are told.
The rest of his teachings show that Jesus could not have meant this.
He consistently opposed religious structures that impose rigid understandings on the people. Surely Jesus' warnings about blind faith
were not only about the Pharisees. They caution all traditions at all

times and in all cultures about falling into distorted faith-messages. As for Thomas, he had already seen value and should have remained committed to it without needing extraordinary signs.

Jesus' diatribes against the Pharisees are most eloquent on this topic: "Woe to you blind guides. Woe to you hypocrites! You blind guides who strain at a gnat and swallow a camel" (Matthew 23:24–25). Jesus detailed many misunderstandings that blind guides foist on the people. In this context he also said, "Call no one your father or teacher" (Matthew 23:9). Ultimately, we are not to turn to other human agents for our answers, but only to God.

The Buddha. Sariputta, the Buddha's chief disciple, one day said, "I have the very deepest faith in you. There has never been another Buddha like you, nor will there ever be. Also there is no person more exalted in enlightenment than you are." The Buddha was not impressed. He asked Sariputta if he knew all the previous Buddhas and all those to come, and also if he truly knew just how free he (the Buddha) was. Sariputta had to admit that he did not have first-hand knowledge of these things. The Buddha replied, "How then can you so boldly claim faith in things of which you do not have understanding?"[2] He chided Sariputta for blind faith and encouraged him to take care that his faith be well founded.

Sometimes people of blind faith try to teach others. The Buddha strongly condemned teaching anything one has not directly experienced. He said, "As when a string of blind men are clinging one to the other such is their talk — also like building a staircase with no idea where it is going or if it is going anywhere." He called all of this "foolish talk."[3] Jesus said similarly that when the blind lead the blind, both fall into the pit (Matthew 15:14).

FORCES ENCOURAGING BLIND FAITH

Conformity. We conform to the beliefs and behaviors of those who cared for us in our early years. Even without explicit education, we take on the positions of people who "had hold of our heads" when we were young and vulnerable. Pressure to conform may be subtle but has strong effects. We maintain some opinions simply because we dare not question or examine them.

Because we are taught to honor "the faith of our fathers," many people think it disrespectful or sinful to examine beliefs. "Behind many beliefs stand memories of beloved persons who taught us these beliefs and who had a stake in our loyalty to them."[4] This is not a sufficient reason to retain a belief. Following established usage and conforming to existing common customs is the easy course. We run the risk, however, of becoming "one among many leading an easy life, clinging to old forms or outmoded ideas at the expense of personal dignity and authenticity."[5]

People who question common religious beliefs are often made to feel that something is wrong with *them* rather than with what they question. Freud said doubters are likely to be told one of three things. First: that the teachings deserve belief because their ancestors believed them. Next: that religious leaders have proof or that proof is in the sacred writings — the very things that are often what is being doubted. Finally: that they are sinful to question the authenticity of religious beliefs.[6]

Authority. For help in deciding what to believe, people rely on authorities. The first authorities are usually parents; often they teach us that any established authority necessarily knows more than we know. We gradually realize that other people have different authorities with opposing claims. Once most people accept an authority or have one imposed on them, however, they find it hard to relinquish its hold. We become very vulnerable to our authorities.

Psychologists have found that people willingly inflict atrocities on others when an accepted authority orders them to do so.[7] This should not surprise us, for history reveals multitudes who have killed and tortured when urged to do so by religious leaders. Witness holy wars, crusades, and inquisitions! "When faith is replaced by orthodoxy, the latter demands only obedience. Scepticism has no chance against the craving for authority."[8]

Completely accepting an authority determines a lot about a person's other beliefs. A devout Southern Baptist finds drinking sinful, and a sincere believer in papal authority considers contraception wrong. People naively accept many unexamined notions on authority, without considering their merits.

St. John of the Cross advised another priest, "If at any time someone, whether superior or anyone else, should try to persuade you of a lax teaching, even though it be confirmed by miracles, do not believe or embrace it."[9] A salty Catholic nun once said to me of religious authorities, "If they say something that makes sense, listen to them. When they talk nonsense, don't." This healthy stance does not come easily to many people.

Personal need. What kind of person follows so blindly? Eric Hoffer identified some bases of blind faith. People who need simplistic solutions to the problems of living are obvious choices. Hoffer also sees a connection between dissatisfaction with oneself and a proneness to credulity. "The urge to escape our real self is also an urge to escape the rational and the obvious."[10] Blind faith does not judge the effectiveness of a doctrine "by its profundity, sublimity or the validity of the truths it embodies, but by how thoroughly it insulates the individual from his self and the world as it is."[11]

Most people are vulnerable to the persuasions of blind faith when caught at the "right time" in their lives. We all have periods when we are more likely to fall for the appeal of having someone else do all our thinking, planning, and choosing for us. Those who want this kind of protection will find it. Such desires hold some people in very tightly controlled religious structures as long as these institutions adequately meet their childish needs.

UNDERSTANDING BLIND FAITH

Institutional bases of blind faith. Sri Aurobindo explained how religious traditions impose blind faith on their followers. Religions want to bind together the faithful and mark them off from an unregenerated outer world. They develop hierarchies, fixed and unprogressive ethical understandings, "crystallized dogmas, ostentations, ceremonials, sanctified superstitions, an elaborate machinery for the salvation of [humanity]. The Church takes the place of the Spirit and a formal subscription to its creed, rituals and order is the thing universally demanded."[12]

This Asian perspective shows us how we look to much of the non-Christian world. Sri Aurobindo also shows us how easily perversion of the religious intention occurs. He says that once past the early church, religious history has almost entirely consisted of rites and ceremonies, authority and church government, and dogmas and beliefs. "Witness the whole external religious history of Europe, that strange sacrilegious tragi-comedy of discords, sanguinary disputations, 'religious' wars, persecutions, State churches and all else that is the very negation of the spiritual life."[13]

Recognizing blind faith. Luther described a willingly blind faith. "So tenaciously should we cling to the world revealed by the Gospel, that were I to see all the Angels of Heaven coming down to me to tell me something different, not only would I not be tempted to doubt a single syllable, but I would shut my eyes and stop my ears, for they would not deserve to be either seen or heard."[14]

The Catholic Index of Forbidden Books echoed such sentiments.[15] In one of my frequent childhood arguments about religion with my father, he showed me an article in *Our Sunday Visitor* newspaper. A priest was extolling the beauty of having the Index. He proclaimed eternal gratitude for it because it protected him from exposure to anything that might disturb his faith. I cried out to my father, "But that's not intellectually honest!" My father responded, "If you valued your faith as Father does his, you would think the same as he does."[16]

PROBLEM CASES OF BLIND FAITH

Abraham is often presented as a perfect example of faith. He was willing to sacrifice his child's life when he heard God order this. Do we really want to listen to every interior voice that speaks to us? One man, first told by God to sacrifice his art collection by burning it, complied with this request. When God next asked him to sacrifice his mother, he missed when he first shot at her. He was then put into psychiatric care.[17] Compare this story with Genesis 22. Yet Abraham, who believed the inner voice of his probable ambivalence about fatherhood, is lauded as the "father of all who believe" (Romans 4:20).[18]

Appeals to blind faith deliberately discourage reason. The cry of Rudolf Hess when swearing in the Nazi party in 1934 was, "Do not seek Adolf Hitler with your brains; all of you will find him with the strength of your hearts."[19] Similarly, those who followed Charles Manson spoke of his charismatic personal appeal that encouraged them to put careful consideration aside.[20]

In specifically religious settings, the holocausts of the members of the People's Temple of Jim Jones[21] and, more recently, of the disciples of David Koresh stand out. Both of these highly charismatic men had a tremendously strong emotional appeal for their followers. Both also made claims that most people would consider blatantly irrational. Both encouraged followers to call them Jesus.

Sri Aurobindo said that people who opt for blind faith will find a controlling religion imposed on them. Such religion "does not base its dogma and practice upon a living sense of ever verifiable spiritual Truth, but on the letter of an ancient book, the infallible dictum of a Pope, the tradition of a Church, the learnèd casuistry of schoolmen and Pundits, conclaves of ecclesiastics, heads of monastic orders, doctors of all sorts."[22] Sri Aurobindo considered all of these to be tribunals that do not allow any questioning, whose sole function is to judge and pronounce. He said they do not think searching, testing, proving, inquiring, or discovery necessary or even allowable. Such arrangements are very satisfying for those who are unwilling to open their eyes and see for themselves.

RELINQUISHING BLIND FAITH

Both Sri Aurobindo and Radhakrishnan pointed out that the Buddha urged people to relinquish unhealthy blind faith in their legalistic, ritualistic Vedic religion. Vedanta then followed the Buddha, effecting a counter-reform. The Christ came when Mosaic law was convicted of narrowness and had become a convention. The Protestant Reformation set right some problems in Christian life, and a Catholic Counter-Reformation then followed.[23] The Buddha, Zoroaster, Socrates, Jesus, Mohammed, Nanak, and Kabir all had to face an inevitable breakaway from traditional views. So, also, "we have to protect the enduring substance of religion from the forms and institutions which suffer from [human] weaknesses and the corruptions of time."[24]

We must not stop with knowing these historical situations, but must continue to recognize when the corrections themselves fall into flaws. "When the established *Shastra*[25] ceases to be a living thing and degenerates or stiffens into a mass of customs and conventions, a new truth, a more perfect law of living has become imperative."[26] A time comes when an honest person has to question authority and raise issues like "But is it really so? How shall I know that this is the truth of things and not superstition and falsehood? When did God command it, or how do I know that this was the sense of [God's] command and not your error or invention, or that the book on which you found yourself is [God's] word at all, or that [God] has ever spoken [God's] will?"[27]

If we want to preserve institutional religion in its familiar forms at all costs, then suppressing questioners as destructive agents perilous to the religious tradition is right. But those who feel called "to destroy falsehood and lay bare a new foundation of truth"[28] must take a stand when they encounter anything that is wrong. All great advances in religious and spiritual understanding come from someone's courageous questioning.

EVALUATING AND REBUILDING FAITH

Echoing the criterion of Jesus (Matthew 7:20), psychologist William James insisted that faith be evaluated according to its fruits, not the roots from where it came.[29] He said this gives us two main criteria: philosophical reasonableness and moral helpfulness.[30] We must exercise what Buddhists call "wise consideration" in evaluating faith stances. A Buddhist dialogue describes positively fruitful faith.

" 'What is the mark of faith?' 'Faith makes serene and it leaps forward.' 'How does faith make serene?' 'When faith arises it arrests the hindrances,[31] and the heart becomes free of them, clear, serene, and undisturbed.' 'How does faith leap forward?' 'When an earnest seeker sees the hearts and minds of others set free, that one leaps forward in aspiration and tries to attain the yet unattained.' "[32] When our faith produces fruits like these — greater purity of heart and ever deeper commitment to spiritual growth — we can trust such faith.

Chapter 8

FAITH IS NOT NARROW

THE PERVERSIONS OF FAITH

When the intellect is originally no larger than a pin's head, and cherishes ideas of God of corresponding smallness, the result, notwithstanding the heroism put forth, is on the whole repulsive.

— WILLIAM JAMES[1]

The man seated next to me on the plane watched me working on this manuscript. He finally said, "Everybody needs to believe in something. Put that in your book." We do need explanations for our lives. We need frameworks of meaning so our lives do not aimlessly drift.

How we hold our beliefs has important consequences. Sri Aurobindo taught that everything depends on the nature of our faith. "If [one] has an ignorant faith and inapt will, [one] will reach nothing true and will fall away to [one's] lower nature. If [one] is lured by false lights, [one] can be carried away by self-will into bypaths that may lead to morass or precipice."[2] Faith is subject to misuse.

BELIEF-INDUCED DISTORTIONS OF REALITY

An unfortunate consequence of faith is its perversions. We can hold our faith in distorted, or even seriously disturbed, ways. This comes from a wrong approach to faith. When we cling to narrow views, our ability to test the factuality and helpfulness of our beliefs falters seriously.

Superstition. Superstitions come from attributing causes to events according to wishes or chance occurrences, and not reason. Popular religious opinion often fosters and encourages superstition within its own group, while considering similar behavior in other traditions erratic.

Some superstitions try to manipulate or "buy off" God. People with a utilitarian attitude toward religion — concern with what they can get out of it — easily fall into superstitions. "A $2 bill had been tucked under a candlestick on the altar of a college chapel. An engineering student, worried about a girl, thought that bribery of the Deity might help."[3]

Sometimes the line between faith and superstition is faint. One Eastern thinker said that "reverence for authority which excludes free investigation turns religion itself into a superstition."[4] We listen to authorities, but must assume personal responsibility for how we use what they give us. To hold that someone else can magically give us the answers is superstitious. Once, when I was lunching with a Jesuit priest,[5] a waitress who had been hovering nearby finally approached him. "Father, some people said you can't really prove that God exists. That's not true, is it?" she asked pleadingly. He smiled benignly and said, "Of course you can prove that God exists; I've done it hundreds of times myself." She went away satisfied; he had served her apparent need at that time.

Differential interpretation. We often honor certain practices in our own religion but consider similar ones of other people superstitious. Many Christians who randomly open the Bible, believing that God will lead them to a helpful passage, consider astrology, which works on the same principle, superstition. A church prayer meeting for rain is considered quite different from a Native American rain dance. Consulting the *I Ching*[6] is superstitious, but "setting out the fleece" (Judges 6:37–40) — asking the Judeo-Christian God for a sign — is not. People told to reject occult interpretations of life events may be encouraged to believe that AIDS is a divine punishment.

Intellectualizing. Intellectualization turns faith into a cognitive exercise. It tries to reduce the living mystery of faith to mental activity. Some people feel that they must build an elaborate system of thought, with no loopholes in it, around faith. They struggle to make their faith fit certain ways of thinking. While faith must not be blatantly *irrational,* we must allow it to be gently *non*-rational. Faith must not go against reason but ought not be constrained to the methods of reason. "The attempt to demonstrate by purely intellectual processes the truth of the deliverances of direct religious experience is absolutely hopeless."[7]

"One confronts a problem; one lives a mystery. A problem permits a number of solutions; a mystery permits only some form of acceptance and stirs us to commitment."[8] Sometimes religions encourage us to reduce the living mystery of faith to mental activity. People struggling to make their thinking fit preconceived ideas may come to very distorted understandings of faith.

Assumptions. Most of us are consciously aware of only a small amount of what we believe. We accept much as true that we never question. These underlying assumptions are usually grounded in emotional needs that hamper living a full life of faith. Spiritual seekers need to examine their beliefs and to ferret out hidden assumptions.

We often ignorantly and inappropriately act upon our unquestioned assumptions. All the good Catholic mothers in my childhood neighborhood tried to disrupt my friendship with a Jewish girlfriend. They said it was bound to affect my faith adversely.

We state most of our beliefs categorically. We say things like "The Pope can speak infallibly" or "The devil is constantly tempting me to get angry" or "Jesus is the only divine incarnation." "We might reasonably preface each of these propositions by the words, 'I believe.' Every proposition becomes in fact a judgment. We take our judgments seriously."[9] Recognizing implicit beliefs helps us see how we color our beliefs to suit emotions or needs. Examining our reactions when someone attacks favorite notions helps us see these dark pockets in our minds.

DOCTRINAL INVITATIONS TO BIGOTRY

Devout Christian psychologist Gordon Allport said that some religious beliefs contain theological invitations to bigotry.[10] While religions preach universal love, their teachings often have exactly opposite effects.

Revelation. Doctrines of revelation claim exclusive possession of God's truth and authority to interpret it. This justifies, as a service to God, mistreating dissenters seen as threats to the common good. Aggressive proselytizing, denying other people freedom of conscience, even torture and death are inflicted — all to save souls! One of my all-time favorite cartoons shows a Crusader high on a big white horse, holding his spear at the throat of an Arab spread-eagled on the ground. The caption reads: "Suddenly I'm very interested in this Christianity of yours. Tell me more."[11]

Election. Doctrines of election even more clearly divide an in-group from out-groups. If the deity has specially chosen some people as the only saved ones or as special agents for God's work, surely their opinions should prevail! They are, after all, *God's* chosen people. If God has chosen, who can argue? Some people never stop to ask what kind of god would "play favorites" in this way.

Theocracy. Allport's final invitation to bigotry is theocracy — having one group's religious opinions and moral standards be the law of the land. This mentality leads to holy wars and legal persecution of dissenters. It weds nationalistic and religious interests and invokes God's name to justify exercising often cruel control over others. A contemporary example of theocracy is the death threat that Muslim authorities, who consider his writings disrespectful of their religion, imposed on writer Salman Rushdie. Because many Muslims around the world believe that killing him would do God a favor, Rushdie has lived in hiding for years.

Even where there is no state church, theocratic tendencies arise. People use the legal system of democracies to impose their religious views on other citizens. "Antiabortion laws, state regulations against the open saloon, and statutes against pornography are only a few examples of the process whereby one group of devotees prescribes its beliefs to the community as a whole, complete with legal sanctions."[12] The point is not that one should endorse abortion, drinking, and pornography, but that faith should be sufficiently broad, confident, and fair to allow other people freedom of conscience about debated issues. Sometimes we want religious freedoms for ourselves that we are not willing to extend to those who differ with us.

When a church cannot impact a state's legal system, it often finds other ways to control its members. Inquisitions are a major theocratic tool. The Catholic Church's silencing of members who disagree with formal church doctrine has been ongoing over the centuries. Years of struggle followed the attempt of some Catholics to get the church to discuss sexual morality openly — the infamous *New York Times* ad! Many Catholic sisters were vigorously persecuted and some communities torn apart by differing opinions about the attempt. Wherever there is no room for dissent and discussion, theocratic structures are usually in force.

MISPLACED STRIVING IN FAITH

Compartmentalizing. Compartmentalizing tightly distinguishes between the sacred and the secular. Faith, however, cannot exist in a vacuum. It cannot be carefully limited to particular times and places or to certain aspects of life. Psychologist Maslow deplored "those who define religion just as going to a particular building on Sunday and hearing a particular kind of formula repeated [and] in terms of ceremonies, or rituals, or dogmas."[13] Compartmentalists may be "Sunday Christians" who conduct the rest of their lives divorced from what they profess on Sunday. They are not people of truly effective faith.

Fanaticism. "It is not faith but fanaticism that asserts that one's own revelation contains all the truth about God that has ever been made known in the past and that no further truth ever will or can be made known in the future."[14] Eric Hoffer understood the benefits fanatics get from their extremism. He said that they see in their passionate attachment the source of all virtue and strength. Although fanatics' single-minded dedication is a "holding on for dear life," they see themselves as supporters and defenders of the holy cause to which they cling. "The fanatic is convinced that the cause he [or she] holds on to is monolithic and eternal — a rock of ages."[15]

Many people who deplore fanatic groups like those of Jim Jones or David Koresh do not realize how similar they are to the early history of many established faiths.[16] Some traditionally religious people even yearn "for the days when people *really* believed, when they cared enough to persecute or form inquisitions or go on crusades. Real belief, in such terms, must be absolutist."[17] Eastern wisdom warns, "When we adopt an absolutist faith, we will not produce free spirits but only men and women of fanatical fervor."[18]

At a recent lay Christian meeting, I overheard one woman proclaiming, "Jesus wants a really virile church, like it used to be, not all the wimpish language people are trying to use now." She offered prayer petitions that use of inclusive language in liturgy be defeated and that the church search out heretics.[19]

People who strongly need very simple solutions to life are easy prey for totalitarian movements — religious or otherwise. Unsettled social conditions that do not meet people's needs for stability, structure, and meaning also support fanatical solutions. Conversions to narrowly defined religions go up when economic times are hard.[20]

Psychologist William James described another face of fanaticism. "Loyalty carried to a convulsive extreme [by] an intensely loyal and narrow mind idealizes the devotion itself."[21] Many pious practices have a fanatic element. One Catholic devotional group keeps vigils in church so that Jesus in the tabernacle will not get lonesome!

Seeking purity. All time-proven religions require that we care about and try to avoid known harmful behavior. Some people, however, seek an unreasonable perfection. They believe it possible to effect in themselves the deep transformation that can come only from spiritual surrender. Some of these people trap themselves in masochistic asceticism. Fear of possible future punishment makes them feel like they *must* suffer. Some so strongly need to suffer that they have no peace unless they are tormenting themselves. Asceticism becomes pathological when "we have morbid melancholy and fear, and the sacrifices made are to purge out sin, and to buy safety."[22]

Masochistically religious people are very self-centered. "One takes pride in the battle fought against the self. One falls into an obsessive dread of the good, so that all the good things that do come to one are self-righteously taxed by guilt."[23] The early psychoanalyst Theodor Reik believed such people always play to an audience. "Even for the solitary monks who subjected themselves to the most terrible flagellations, there was the one and all-important witness: God."[24]

Miracle-seeking. Many people wanting some taste of spiritual nectar look wherever they think they may find it. The loudest signals come from the blatantly miraculous. The New Age "spirituality supermarket" offers some extreme examples of supernaturalism, such as channeling, esoteric healing, and visionary cults. Yet Christianity is not without its own versions. How many Catholics flock unwittingly to every newly alleged appearance of the Virgin Mary? How many Protestants clamor for healing and other miracles from their televangelists and revival leaders?

For some people, faith becomes a quest for special experiences. They seek visions, miracles, or other extraordinary phenomena to support belief. Rather than *being* faith, such activities are really quite contrary to faith. They are attempts to hold on to something tangible instead of resting in the darkness of faith. When Thomas said he would believe only if he could put his hand into Jesus' side, Jesus told him his understanding was wrong (John 20:29). We are not to look to physical signs for confirmation.

John of the Cross considered such seeking very dangerous.[25] His bottom line is that we should never attach *any* importance to such experiences and that any genuine ones are for the good of others rather than ourselves. John warns that emphasizing the supernatural leads us to deceive ourselves and others. We will see only what comforts us and may misuse whatever is genuine in such experiences because of our desires. We will rely on signs and wonders rather than bare faith. Such experiences also can lead us into vain self-importance.

Other-worldliness. Most people who retreat from active life to devote themselves to spiritual work express genuinely religious values. Many spiritual traditions deeply honor this monastic calling. Some people, however, try to flee from involvement in the real problems of life by embracing all-absorbing religious practices. Religious faith does offer such cop-out options, and one need not seek a cloister to find them. Psychologist James said an "imaginative absorption in the love of God to the exclusion of all practical human interests" is "theopathic." He considered this most common "where devoutness is intense and the intellect feeble."[26]

A CONCLUSION

A faith intention can go awry in many different ways. This causes suffering both to the believer and those affected by his or her misplaced emphases. All traditions have produced saints and religious geniuses; all also have had people who fall short of healthy religiousness. Integrated faith can give genuine meaning to life. Worthy faith produces serenity instead of worry, productive striving rather than guilt or excesses, loving concern for others, and the ability to commit to chosen values.

Chapter 9

FAITH IS NOT EXCLUSIVE

TOWARD UNIVERSAL PERSPECTIVES

===

The different religions are like various languages in which God
has spoken.

— SARVEPALLI RADHAKRISHNAN[1]

This chapter looks at the difficulties involved when we close our
hearts to seeing truth in the religious ideas and experiences of others.
In a shrinking world of growing psychological sophistication, doing
so becomes increasingly difficult. Yet many people persistently need
to see their own faith tradition as different, apart from, or truer than
others.

Radhakrishnan said we must realize that any given way of ex-
pressing spiritual truth is relative, so it cannot have a unique value
that excludes other forms. None can be the only possible way to express the truths it offers. Because of its limits each way necessarily
leaves something outside of itself.[2] We can find that "something" in
other time-proven traditions.

Christian monk Abhishiktananda wrote that we must consider
it possible that other traditions have an authentic faith. Only such
openness makes us able to suspend wrongful judgment of them and
truly respect them. Without this attitude, we cannot see what hidden wisdom they hold. He optimistically felt that people *can* be
open; "there is no doubt that any believer with a minimum of
spiritual intelligence can do this."[3]

83

CLOSED FAITH SYSTEMS

How we experience and interpret our lives depends upon how we live them. When we cannot participate in the spiritual consciousness of another tradition, we may insist that only our own position is true. Because we have given only this solution a chance to validate itself, we consider others in error.

The scourge of close-mindedness. At the beginning of the last century, Christian missionary Bishop Reginald Heber illustrated such closedness when he said:

> The heathen in his blindness
> Bows down to wood and stone.[4]

Heber saw only what was happening on the surface; he had no understanding of Hindu spirituality and no capacity to participate in Hindu experience and consciousness. More bluntly, he simply did not know what he was talking about. He had closed his mind to all but one faith choice.

The documents of Vatican II specifically urge Catholics to be open to the truth in traditions predating the Christian one.[5] However, many people consider such openness to other traditions a threat to their own faith. They close themselves off and dig deep protective trenches around their religious beliefs. They think that if someone who differs from them is right in any way, then they must be wrong — and that is an intolerable thought! They view other traditions as somehow being in competition with their own, like a rival sports team.

Against narrow perspectives. Eastern thought tells us that dogmas used without fear or attachment can truly aid us in our spiritual work and help us teach the path to others. Many people, however, cling to doctrine, unable to manifest such freedom. Jesuit Thomas Hand pointed out that "from an eastern point of view the glorification of theology in the west is a great and serious obstacle to seeing."[6]

When we narrowly identify ourselves with divisive nouns of religious affiliation, we put barriers between ourselves and others who seek the truth as we do. One "cannot be both a Christian and a

Muslim at the same time. The nouns keep us apart."[7] Furthermore, we seem to forget that Jesus was not a Christian, and the Buddha was not a Buddhist. However, all seekers should be christian (anointed), muslim (surrendered), and buddhist (fully awakened), and so on.

When we finally reach our goal, at the highest level, "it is true that [even the] adjectives dissolve. For all dissolves when we meet God face to face."[8] All theology "must eventually fade in the light of transconceptual reality."[9] Realizing this can help us appreciate openness. We also can remember that Jesus rebuked his disciples for trying to prevent others from offering spiritual succor. "Whoever is not against us, is for us" (Mark 9:40, Luke 9:50).

A PATH TO OPENNESS

Beyond triumphalism. Another Jesuit, Aloysius Pieris, named special enemies to understanding: "Catholic triumphalism based on ecclesiolatry (no salvation outside the church) and Protestant fundamentalism based on bibliolatry (no revelation outside the Bible)."[10] Pieris called both of these positions idolatries that ought have no place in genuine faith. The intransigent evangelism they spawn speaks poorly of Christian faith.

Seiichi Yagi, a Buddhist convert to Christianity whose theology drew together notions from both traditions, came to some important conclusions. "The absolute claim of Christianity is grounded in the insistence that Jesus Christ alone is the revelation of God. *Extra ecclesiam nulla salus* [outside the church there is no salvation]. From this, religion must be understood as an impossible attempt by human beings to take possession of the truth."[11]

This author argued that Jesus takes his place alongside other venerable gifts of God to lead people to spiritual understanding. Yagi held that his theology makes it possible "that the claim of absoluteness by Christianity can be eliminated."[12] He said that his understanding of Jesus lets "our concept of the activated Self ('Christ in me') . . . be compared to the concept of Buddhahood."[13] Radhakrishnan said similarly that both the Buddha and the Christ indicate the universal reality appearing in a human manifestation. "The Absolute is reflected in the relative. Each manifestation is unique, is a relative Absolute."[14]

In saying such, these scholars elaborated what documents of Vatican II urge. These church teachings tell us to respect and make use of the ways in which God spoke to people in the venerable Eastern traditions before the coming of Jesus.[15] Some more traditional voices have spoken similarly. Origen taught, "There exist diverse forms of the Word under which It reveals itself."[16] St. Thomas Aquinas perhaps put it the most simply: "Wise people do not worry about names."[17]

Seeing our limits. Jesuit Pieris discusses how strongly Greek culture influenced Christianity. He says this refined and pervasive culture would not allow any outside religion or philosophy to affect it substantially. Greece allowed itself to be somewhat Christianized only because Christianity allowed itself to be Hellenized. He concluded, "Hellenism, therefore, remains the door as well as the barrier for any non-Christian religion to make a fresh contribution to Western theology."[18] Perhaps, with good will, we can overcome this barrier.

We judge by externals only if we think something must be cast into familiar words or images in order to be true. Different religions exist precisely because cultures and times differ. Abhishiktananda gave guidelines for being able to perceive familiar truths in unfamiliar garments. "We have no right to forget that the mental climate of both the Semitic and the Greco-Roman worlds was quite different from that of ancient India. We have to put on one side everything which is not the actual experience we are trying to understand."[19]

Those in other traditions sometimes seem closed to us. To understand, Abhishiktananda invited us to enter into their views — views that are not without basis. "It is necessary for the Christian to feel in his soul the agony of the Hindu who cannot see how Christianity, with all its dogmatic formulae, its institutions and rituals, can truly be compatible with profound inner experience."[20] Such experience is the core of the great Eastern traditions of Buddhism and Hinduism.

OPENING THE HEART

A personal opening. Initially, I was frighteningly close-minded about other traditions. When students first begged me to hear a Hindu yogi speak, I declined for some time. I thought, "I am a Christian. What can any pagan teach me?" I finally became convinced that faith that must be treated like a hothouse flower is no faith worth having. As I began to investigate various traditions, I increasingly saw value in them as I grew more willing to see.

If ever we interpret religious experiences in any tradition's terms, that tradition becomes validated for us. I speak from personal experience. I have found the interpretive systems of many traditions equally adequate to explain spiritual experience. They are also equally capable of binding us with the force of conviction that intense spiritual experience brings.

An early ecumenist. A nineteenth-century Hindu saint, Ramakrishna, led the way in such experiments. After he realized union with God as his beloved Divine Mother, a Sufi initiated him into Islam. "I began to repeat the holy name of Allah. After three days I realized the goal of that form of devotion."[21] Later, Ramakrishna became interested in Christianity and studied the Bible. A vision of Jesus held him spellbound for three days. Then Jesus came toward him, embraced him, and merged into him. Ramakrishna concluded: "It is the same God [found] along different paths."[22]

Unless we have the openness of a Ramakrishna, we can never fully experience another tradition, nor can we understand it. Since all the time-proven traditions offer much of value, this inability is a real loss. We usually celebrate when someone shows openness to our own tradition, but fear being open ourselves to other paths. When we wish to fully embrace truth, this attitude puts us in a real bind. We cannot genuinely explore other spiritual paths if we dread losing something by opening our minds to their possibilities.

Starting to open. Leonard Swidler says that we need to approach other people "of differing views with the primary purpose of *learning*, not teaching." He claims that the capital sin is not pride, but the sloth of taking the easy way out, of remaining intellectually and spiritually stagnant. "A major means of dialogue is a self-critical attitude toward ourself and our tradition. A lack of self-criticism will mean there is no valid sincerity, no true honesty, no authentic integrity."[23]

Abhishiktananda explains the minimum openness necessary. "The Upanishads[24] will remain completely incomprehensible so long as [one] does not approach them with at least of a minimum of faith, of sensitivity to what is interior and spiritual."[25] He admits that he and his colleagues felt some fear when they began exploring other traditions. "It seemed at times that some of us sensed a real danger of losing their faith through a too close contact with the Upanishads — as though a real and genuine faith could be so easily lost!"[26] He finally concluded that, as the first epistle of John (4:18) teaches, "fear is incompatible with a deeply rooted faith in and love of Christ."[27]

THE VIEW FROM THE TOP

A personal experience. My father is quite dismayed because I "hang out with heathens" and wants to bring me back to his truth. He said, "Say you ask me how to get to Chicago, and I tell you to go down this road until you reach the stop-light, then turn left. You will never get to Chicago if you turn right." Interestingly, he is wrong. Given enough time and persistence, a person would eventually get to Chicago. The analogy for the spiritual life is compelling. If we take wrong turns, we can still get home; however, it entails a lot of suffering and requires patience.

My reply left him temporarily speechless, but he still has not given up. I said, "When you are climbing a mountain and realize that you're on a path leading to the top, it's very tempting to call out to others off to your side to come on over where you are. You're so sure you've found the only path that leads up. However, someone sitting on top of the mountain can see that all the roads lead up." This Eastern answer recognizes both the validity of different choices and the limits that life experience puts on the choices available to any one person.[28] Such a perspective lets us see faith as seeking the Ultimate Reality in some particular way among various options.

Celebrating unity in multiplicity. Radhakrishnan argued that exaggerating doctrinal differences between traditions overlooks their common basis. We find that the diversity of dogmatic interpretations tends to diminish as we climb up the ladder of spiritual perfection. "If we leave aside the secondary interpretations, we find that the seers make practically the same report about the nature of Absolute Reality."[29]

Radhakrishnan excellently taught appreciation of the common core in religious teachings. He said, "Resemblances in higher religions are to be welcomed as the expressions of the working of the mysterious spirit of God at sundry times and in diverse manners."[30] He strongly argued that the higher religions tend toward convergence. To see this, we need only look at the spiritual facts on which they are based and the moral universalism that they teach. Thus, "we can draw inspiration from more than one of the existing religions."[31]

Other Western voices. Christian ecumenism is not something new. Fifteenth-century cardinal Nicholas de Cusa hoped that "by means of a few sages versed in the variety of religions that exist throughout the world it could be possible to reach a certain peaceful concord."[32] Two centuries earlier, Franciscan layman Ramon Lull said, "Our discussions should continue as long as necessary until we arrive at one faith and one religion so that we will have a form of honoring each other and serving each other."[33]

Eighteenth-century Protestant mystic William Law wrote, "There is not one [way] for the Jew, another for a Christian and a third for the heathen. No: God is one, human nature is one, salvation is one, and the way to it is one; that is the desire of the soul turned to God."[34] Nor do we have any special monopoly on faith and goodness. Berdyaev was a teacher of activist saint Dorothy Day. He said that Hindus, Buddhists, Jews, Muslims, and free thinkers "if they strive after God, the spiritual life, truth and goodness, may be much nearer to God and Christ than the outward adepts of Christianity."[35]

IN SUMMARY

We can more easily respect others if we put the focus on choice and values when we consider faith rather than on personal certainty and security. Why should we care to respect values and choices other than those we have adopted? First, it offers others the respect and freedom that we want for ourselves. However, it goes beyond that. The ancient Greek roots of the word "ecumenism" meant "household management."[36] How long will it take us to realize that we are, indeed, one household, one family, one body of the Christ, one Buddha-nature, one Self that is the All?[37]

Our world is terribly, desperately in need of spiritual perspectives on life. If those who consider themselves spiritually invested contend with each other over the cultural and historical differences that have shaped different vehicles for spiritual truths, there seems little hope. When we unite in appreciation of each other, then all who care — regardless of tradition — can bond together to combat with love the common "enemies" of indifference and spiritual insensitivity.[38]

Part III

A FAITH THAT
SERVES WELL

Chapter 10

FAITH IS A CHOICE

HAVING IT "BE SO"

At some minute I did answer *Yes* to Someone — or Something — and from that hour my life, in self-surrender, had a goal.

— Dag Hammarskjöld[1]

In his early life, my favorite psychologist William James suffered intense depressions and occasionally was suicidal. While studying in Europe during his twenties, he made a startling diary entry: "My first act of free will shall be to believe in free will."[2] With this choice, James took responsibility for his life. His depressions continued, but he was never again suicidal.

To decide you will believe something — what a very interesting statement! But James went further yet. He said that belief and choice are essentially the same thing. Holding something to be true or choosing it — both are simply letting something "be so" for oneself.[3]

We can reword this in our terminology of faith and belief. In a faith choice, this "being so" is a commitment; we act in such a way as to ensure its "being so." With any belief, religious or other, we cognitively see something as "being so" — whether it factually is so or not. Belief does not necessarily engage us as faith does.

FAITH, BELIEF, AND CHOICE

James said choices have three characteristics. First, they are either possible or impossible. Possible ones are then forced or unforced, and momentous or trivial.[4]

Possible and impossible beliefs. If I know that I have put only $3 in my purse, I cannot — if I am sane — hold it to be $300. Religious beliefs, however, are not usually subject to such reality constraints. Our early training, the accident of where we were born, the bent of our temperament, our early emotional conditioning, the opinions of others around us — all these make holding some religious positions very easy and possible for us and embracing others very difficult.

For example, had you been born in southern India, strongly inclined toward devotional religion, you would likely feel an intense love of Krishna, the usual devotional object there. You would have a very real relationship with this incarnation of Vishnu, second person of a Hindu trinity, and Jesus would feel foreign to you. Similarly, people reared either as Muslim or Christian usually have difficulty finding other traditions believable. However, our religious attitudes are not as fixed and immutable as they initially seem to be. People *can* open to values in other traditions.

Momentous and trivial choices. The distinction between momentous and trivial choices is obvious. How I dress my salad tonight is ultimately a trivial choice because it has few implications for my future life. All decisions about faith are momentous because they deal with our ultimate good and the meaningfulness of life.

Forced and avoidable decisions. Faith decisions, like ones regarding human relationships, are also forced. We cannot avoid them. I can forever avoid deciding whether I prefer strawberry or peach ice cream, but my every action affects faith choices. Trying to put off choice may make faith very difficult later. Since deferring decision may incline me to do things opposed to faith, I am always deciding even when I try to avoid faith choices.

FAITH CHOICES

Bases of choosing. Psychologist Erik Erikson said, "Trust born of care is the touchstone of a given religion."[5] We must have basic trust for religious surrender to feel safe and to develop reverence. Early life experiences powerfully affect our ability to trust. Erikson also held that some religious rituals deal with fear of trusting, sometimes by trying to manipulate God.[6]

Another psychologist of religion said that freedom to choose is limited because each of us is in touch with only a small part of reality. Our own personal histories make our different options "function as love and hate objects."[7] We each choose to embrace what most satisfies us.

Integrated faith requires that we recognize our needs and fears — even see them behind our faith choices — but not let them drive us to inappropriate choices. Whenever we choose out of unexamined or unrecognized fear, habit, or guilt, we may make less suitable choices. We ought not let superstition or security-seeking guide our choices.

Choosing for faith. William James offered a prescription to develop faith: "One need only in cold blood ACT as if the thing in question were real, and keep acting as if it were real, and it will infallibly end by growing into such a connection with our life that it will become real."[8] This is, indeed, what we do whenever we choose to act inside or outside a particular faith vision. Recognizing this process is scary ground for many people. We may be quite willing to see such conditioning in other people's lives, but we do not want to recognize it in our own cherished stances.

Choosing to believe for even a brief experiment can be powerful. Psychology students who have experimented with paranoid thought find it gets a grip on them that is hard to shake. When they choose for a day to interpret everything they see as a sinister plot or act of malevolence directed against them, they find that the effects linger for days. Choosing to see the world as threatening actually turns the world into a threatening place for them.

The Buddha gave guidelines for making good choices. "When you know for yourselves what is unwholesome, blamable, censured by the wise, and undertaken and observed leads to harm and ill, you should abandon it. When you know for yourself what is wholesome, blameless, praised by the wise, and undertaken and observed leads to benefit and happiness, then having undertaken it live by it."[9] Both the Buddha and Jesus taught us to know values by their fruits (Matthew 7:20). Living rightly eventually brings assurance that we are in a right way and will come to good and not ill.

Behavior and faith. Attitudes develop from how we behave. This understanding is behind James's prescription for faith. We also change faith attitudes and beliefs by behavior. If we become accustomed to doing things we were taught are discordant, they bother us less and less. We thus shape and change conscience.

Here is a simple example of the relationship between religious beliefs and behavior. A Baptist student, who came to college convinced that drinking is sinful, liked his roommate who drank. He fell in with his roommate's friends, tried drinking, and soon came to see nothing wrong with it. Those who continue to think drinking is sinful may say that this student "lost" his faith — as if faith were some "thing" that could be accidentally misplaced. The student simply behaved in ways that best fit with another conclusion, and that understanding became more real to him. Behaving contrary to an earlier belief changed his belief.

THE IMPORTANCE OF DECISION

The decisions we make about our options determine what will later be possible or impossible for us. For example, how I behave toward another person makes friendship either possible or impossible. If I choose to be friendly, a friendship might develop. If I ignore the other person because I think that she could never be interested in me or because I am not attracted to her, friendship becomes impossible. Faith in the possibility of friendship sets the conditions that make friendship possible.

Faith decisions. Similarly, religious actions determine our reality regarding any given religious perspective. They shape what can be true for us. If we do not have sufficient faith to begin acting on a value, deeper faith cannot develop. "A fact cannot come at all unless a preliminary faith exists in its coming. Faith in a fact can help create the fact."[10]

Sri Aurobindo worded it even more strongly. "This soul in [us], is, as it were, made of faith, a will to be."[11] Our being becomes whatever our will or faith is. Truths we see and choose to live become for us the truths of our being; we can have no other *real* truth. "We create our own truth of existence in our own action of mind and life."[12]

The right to believe. In spiritual matters, we cannot wait for conclusive proof before deciding what to do. God is not an intellectual problem, cannot be confined to concepts and ideas. Thinking about faith choices pushes words around, but proves nothing. We cannot *know*, but only *act* — either to aspire to God or to forget about it.

Psychologist James said that skeptics prefer to lose out on a possible good because they are unwilling to risk being in error. Those who choose faith are willing to be duped in hope of a great good. "In either case we act, taking our life in our hands. No one of us ought to issue vetoes to the other [or] words of abuse. We ought to respect one another's mental freedom. We have the right to believe at our own risk any hypothesis that is live enough to tempt our will."[13]

Saying "yes." Dag Hammarskjöld's poignant memoirs, *Markings*, beautifully captured choosing for faith in the quotation that opens this chapter. Saying "yes," choosing to make something be "so" for us — this is faith. It may be "yes" to a divine incarnation, "yes" to a spiritual discipline, "yes" to a community's code and rites. The great Vedantist Shankara considered faith to be an orientation of "yes-ness" or "awakeness to transcendence, *the ability to see the point* of a religious tradition."[14]

Whatever our "yes" or "no," we make a choice; the repeated confirmation of that choice in daily life is living faith. This is what that very helpful priest, speaking with the confused young woman I was in my twenties, meant when he said, "Faith is wanting God badly enough that you spend your entire life seeking God." This understanding of faith refers to how we *act*, what we *do*, not to ideas and opinions.

FAITH CREATING REALITY

Faith and the beliefs it produces go beyond making certain future outcomes possible. Strong beliefs of any kind — and the strongest often come from chosen faith stances — can actually determine what that reality will be. The more strongly we hold a belief, the more powerful its effect is.

Effects of choice. In an essay's title, W. C. Smith asked about the Muslim Holy Book, "Is the *Qur'an* (Koran) the Word of God?" Smith answered: "There have been stupid and petty persons, no doubt, on both sides. Each answer [also] has been sustained by persons brilliant, wise, informed, careful, honest, critical, and sincere."[15] This same is true of those who say "yes" or "no" to any religion. Some saints and sinners alike have affirmed any given tradition, while other saints and sinners have chosen not to accept it.

What makes the difference between those who say, "Yes, the *Qur'an* is the word of God" and those who answer "no"? Smith replied: "Those who adopt either position, and follow it through consistently, find their reward. Those who hold the *Qur'an* to be the word of God have found that this conviction leads them to a knowledge of God."[16] What makes the difference is the attitude with which one approaches the *Qur'an* — or the Christian Bible or any other scripture or teaching.

This is also true of other religious attitudes. Sri Aurobindo promised, "Your contact with the Divine Mother will become so intimate that you have only to put everything into her hands to have her present guidance, her direct command or impulse, the sure indication of the thing to be done and the way to do it and the result."[17] Devotees of the Mother *do* experience this. Those who trustingly seek divine guidance — *truly* trusting; one cannot fake effective trust — typically get the guidance they need.

Faith healing. The mind can create physical illness in the body; the mind can even kill. When someone puts a voodoo hex on a staunch believer, it causes severe psychological tension. This interrupts normal self-regulatory physiological processes of the body like blood pressure and osmotic balance. The expected death follows and strengthens onlookers' belief in the power of hexes.[18]

Likewise, if we think we are being given helpful medicine, taking sugar pills can make us well — the placebo effect. Belief makes these powerful changes possible. Faith healing clearly illustrates the potent effects of belief on reality.

A prominent faith healer was asked to pray for three seriously ill women without their knowing she was doing it. Nothing happened. Then the doctor told the women about the healer, built up their trust in her, and said she would pray for them at a certain time. Although the healer did *not* pray at that time, the severe symptoms of all three women showed dramatic improvement.[19] Many research studies support the conclusion that belief can make healing happen. Such belief apparently allows the body and mind to relax so that the body can heal itself of whatever was maintaining the illness.

This should not surprise people who know Christian scripture. How common it was for Jesus to tell people that their faith is what healed them or made them whole! The Bible also says that, because of people's unbelief, Jesus sometimes could not perform miracles.[20] He himself told his disciples that their inability to heal was because of their unbelief (Matthew 17:19–20). Belief shapes reality that powerfully.

IN SUMMARY

A story. A story beautifully illustrates choice that makes possible further faith development.[21] It also shows how action — not certainty or opinion — is the heart of faith. At a conference, a Buddhist monk gave basic meditation instruction. One woman was immediately in great pain during the session but, seeing how still everyone else was sitting, tried hard not to move. She was in agony by the end of the meditation period and was greatly relieved when someone else asked about pain. The monk simply replied, "Oh, yes, the pain." Then someone asked how long he had been meditating, and he answered "twenty years." Finally someone asked him if he believed in God. He sat silently for a moment, then said very slowly: "I believe in — Something." On hearing this, the woman decided that she was very definitely going to experiment with meditation — for at least about twenty years.

A conclusion. We see how very strongly our important choices affect not only the time immediately after choosing, but the rest of our lives. We also see some flexibility in religious choice, that we are not stuck with positions that no longer work for us. We can explore various options and, by acting upon them, encourage those that tempt faith to become real in our lives. What awesome responsibility we have for ourselves!

If we accept that faith is a choice and a risk, we can choose to gamble an entire lifetime seeking loving knowledge of God. We can find some suitable framework within which to live out that choice. Once we have chosen, we must give the option a genuine opportunity to prove itself. What we choose must have time to show us how living with it will affect our lives. Having found a particular teaching worthy of consideration, we enter into a confident experiment with it.

Chapter 11

FAITH IS A CONFIDENT EXPERIMENT

"GAMBLING" WITH OUR LIVES

Faith in the biblical view is an act of the whole personality. It is an act of self-surrender, of obedience.

— PAUL TILLICH[1]

When we want answers to questions that science or ordinary living cannot satisfy, we must look deeper. The Buddha decided to pursue spiritual living when he concluded: "Why, being myself subject to birth, aging, ailment, death, sorrow, and defilement, do I seek after what is also subject to these things?"[2] We may have often asked ourselves the Buddha's question. Why do we keep hankering for what we know will not satisfy us? Trying to find that which is not subject to impermanence and suffering is to embark on a confident experiment in faith. This faith becomes how we live our lives.

We in the West often reify faith, turn it into a "thing." "Our typically modern-Western way [speaks] of faith as if it were something that a person may 'have.' [In the East] faith pertains to *the way in which* one does things."[3] Eastern languages use "faith" as a verb, adjective, or adverb. A saying attributed to St. Augustine comes near to this: "Faith is the power by which commitment is given to intangibles."[4]

THE NEED FOR FAITH

Faith is indispensable in all religious activities. "It is this attitude that gives an action its religious character. [Faith] is the core of all religious endeavor."[5] All the schools of Hindu thought consider faith the basis for its path of salvation. The Venerable Sayadaw U Pandita, head of a major lineage of Theravadan Buddhism, said that all of spiritual life is the awakening and deepening of faith.[6] St. John of the Cross said, "Faith is the only proximate and proportionate means to union with God."[7]

Faith for seeing. Faith is necessary for understanding. It is "prerequisite to ascertaining truth,"[8] and includes the desire, resolve, and commitment to know. Faith rests on deep reverence for the truth that one hopes and wills eventually to attain. This endeavor is not especially linked with intellectual questions. The East understands faith as "taking up of the religious life seriously and genuinely."[9]

Scholar W. C. Smith takes issue with how Christians have understood that faith is necessary for understanding. "To translate *credo ut intelligam* as 'I believe in order that I may understand' makes it seem ridiculous and offensive. 'I become involved, in order that I may understand.' "[10]

Sri Aurobindo similarly taught that faith is a deep will to know and to see, and to do and be according to what we see and know. "If faith is absent, if one trusts to the critical intelligence which goes by outward facts and jealously questions then there is no possibility of living out that greater knowledge."[11]

Faith for becoming. Faith, so understood, "determines by its power the measure of our possibilities of becoming."[12] Acting upon this faith with resolve will enable us to reach the supreme goal. Without such effective faith we can never achieve anything decisive either materially or spiritually. Only by resting on this sure basis and positive support can we ever come to any measure of worldly or spiritual success, satisfaction, and happiness. "The merely sceptical mind loses itself in the void."[13]

Indian scriptures, especially the *Bhagavad Gita*, repeatedly assert that without faith all religious activity is worthless. The Buddha said, "By faith you shall be free and go beyond the realm of death."[14] We have already seen how often Jesus said that the good he brought others was due to their faith.[15] Sri Aurobindo summarized what all these sources say. "This is a truth which has to be lived, not argued out in the mind's darkness. One has to grow into it, one has to become it — that is the only way to verify it."[16]

WRONG APPROACHES TO THE FAITH EXPERIMENT

Clinging. A chief barrier to knowing God is clinging to opinions about God. The author of *The Cloud of Unknowing* urged us not to let any thoughts, no matter how pleasing or consoling, get between us and God. Thinking about God will always be "mixed with some sort of imagination, and be tainted, and [can] lead us into great error."[17]

John of the Cross taught that we can seek the Holy only through emptiness. The fuller we are of particular beliefs or opinions, the less room there is for the Holy to come to us in our meditation or interior prayer. John said, "If we close the eyes of the intellect to earthly and heavenly things we shall remain in faith."[18] Buddhist teachings argue similarly. So we cling to no particular ideas or opinions and remain fully open to what is revealed to us.

Jewish psychologist David Bakan wrote: "Mankind has developed a concept of God with whom he forever plays peekaboo, and through it manages to learn how to manage life. When the day comes that he clings to an image of the ever-present God as the real one, and stops the game of peekaboo with God, then he loses out on the fundamental value of the game."[19]

"Hedging one's bets." In college I was taught Pascal's wager as a quite reasonable approach to faith. Pascal argued that we are safest deciding to act as if God exists. If we are right, there are big payoffs after death and, if we are wrong, we are just dead. On the other hand, if we act as if God does *not* exist, we are in big trouble after death if God *does* exist, and, if not, we are just dead. In the long run, our odds for a good outcome are better if we wager that God exists. I found Pascal's wager despicable when I first heard it. I still do. It has nothing to do with real faith.

Easy answers. The Buddha warned us about taking the easy way out — accepting a position without adequate examination. He listed bases for faith that at first glance might seem good ones. These ways all rest on what someone else says, on claims of authority, or on simple opinion. Our desires support some of them. He concluded that, after our own hard work with a teaching, we ought to examine its fruits.[20] In faith, we work with a teaching that seems worthy. Then we discern; we examine how it affects us to determine its value for us. Answers come later and reflect what we have seen, not what others would have us believe.

What constitutes overly easy answers differs for different people. Some people may need to discard certain religious beliefs that serve other people well. Priest-scholar Panikkar says, "Clearly there remains the major difficulty of ascertaining how satisfactorily [each belief] expresses faith. Certain creedal formulas deriving from a naive, underdeveloped cast of mind may not answer the needs of more highly developed people."[21]

Institution-caused problems. People's first attempts to convert their lives into spiritual living do not often receive sufficient institutional support. These seekers may finally settle for a set system of belief and ethics occasionally touched by spiritual emotion. The outward machinery frequently dominates even that saving element, and the sheltering structure becomes a tomb. Only very few seekers practice genuinely spiritual living. Many of these stay carefully within the often narrow limits prescribed by their tradition. The majority neglect even that puny effort and are content to practice only a simple or mindless piety. In the end "the spirit in the religion has become a thin stream choked by sands."[22]

Abhishiktananda deplored the same situation. He said most Christians have only superficial self-awareness and seem satisfied with that. His criticisms are a potent judgment of the institution. "They are quite content with a Jewish style of ritualism and legalism, with rationalism derived from Greece and a juridical constitution inspired by ancient Rome. They cannot allow themselves to be seized inwardly by the devouring Presence."[23]

FAITHFUL EXPERIMENTING, *SHRADDHA*

The Sanskrit word *shraddha* is variously translated as confidence, faith, devotion, venturing, trust, setting one's heart on, and willingness to risk. It is common to all Hindu spiritual paths. Its Buddhist counterpart in the Pali language, with the same meanings, is *saddha*. This term is quite like the *original* meanings, explained in chapter 2, of the words "faith" and "belief."

Confidence. Setting one's heart on something or someone has various facets such as desire, confidence, and trust.[24] Theravadan Buddhist teachings usually translate *saddha* as confidence. This confidence is wide-ranging. In effective faith it covers the teachings, the teacher, one's circumstances, and oneself — one's own ability and commitment.

A faith choice is intimately bound to hope and desire. It is expecting, being ready for, something that may become our own experience. Being committed to our values and to what we want sustains hope and provides the basis for faith. Vedantist Ramanuja taught that faith presupposes confidence. Trusting that something will prove effective, with faith we then plunge into it. *Shraddha* occurs when we let something we see as worthwhile engage us.[25]

Risking. Theravadan Buddhism strongly emphasizes putting forth courageous effort. This tradition says valiantly working with what we have seen as valuable is indispensable. This necessarily involves risk, for there are no guarantees. Without taking risks we become like the servant who buried his talents rather than investing them (Matthew 25:14–30). Courageous faith "means surrender, not only to reality-up-till-now, but also to reality-from-now-on, including unknown novelties."[26]

Panikkar also writes of risk. "Faith can only be lived, but living it may at times demand risking it in order to remain faithful. The venture hazards a conversion so thoroughgoing that the convictions and beliefs [one] had hitherto held may vanish or undergo a far-reaching change. Unquestionably the venture is perilous; you gamble your life."[27]

Hindu Vedanta called the spiritual path "a razor's edge." Kierkegaard deeply understood this element in Christian faith. "I choose;

that means so much to me that I decide to stake my whole life upon that if. That is called risking; and without risk faith is an impossibility."[28] Faith follows most easily when either hope or desire runs high enough to bring us to surrendered seeking.

Wholeheartedness. Most Eastern teachers emphasize the wholeheartedness that faith requires. *Shraddha* "is not blind belief but the faith which asks whether the outer performance without the living spirit is enough."[29] In perfect faith, our whole being assents either to a truth we have seen or to a truth offered us to which we aspire.[30] Faith can tend toward many different objects. "The term *shraddha* is open, in the sense that it does not itself specify or even suggest what it is on which one puts one's heart."[31] However, without hedging or holding back, we reach out toward that to which we aspire.

Both the Old and New Testaments echo this. Properly religious action calls for heart. "Though I bestow all my goods to feed the poor, and though I give my body to be burned, and have not charity, it profits me nothing" (1 Corinthians 13:3). "I hate, I despise your feasts. Take away from me the noise of your songs; to the melody of your harps I will not listen. But let justice roll down like waters, and righteousness like an ever-flowing stream" (Amos 5:21, 23–24).

Any religious activity in which we partake — sacrificial oblation, donations, austerity, ritual, devotion — "is regarded as vacuous *if one's heart is not in it*."[32] Sri Aurobindo wrote, "Because *shraddha* is the central principle of our existence, any of these things done without *shraddha* is a falsity and has no true meaning or true substance."[33] We can go through the motions without there being real religious intent behind them.

We can accept particular teachings, rituals, and religious obligations, "but grudgingly. To accept it with *shraddha* is to put one's heart in it [and be] pleased that it is so."[34] Recall that St. James said that the devils also believe, but shudder (James 2:19). One can believe without faith, without the wholeheartedness of *shraddha*.

The opposite of wholehearted faith is certainly not disbelief, but rather either indifference or a scattering of concern.[35] The Book of Revelation says just how unacceptable halfhearted endeavor is; "because you are lukewarm, I will spit you out of my mouth" (Revelation 3:16).

A special seeing. Faith's knowing differs from the clarity of the reasoning mind. By faith, one penetrates obscurely into the depths of one's own being and reality. We must realize that here we go beyond the mind's power to explore solely by means of thought and sense-perception.[36] When mystics and seers try to report their experiences, they stutter. We can understand faith's seeing only in the experience of seeing itself; no one can teach it to us.

Hindus have long understood that the supreme knowledge "is not a 'knowing that,' but an immediate knowing of: a direct knowledge of Reality with a large capital R."[37] Buddhists and mystics of all traditions see this similarly. We can consider *shraddha* an influence of the Spirit. "That which receives the influence and answers to the call is not so much the intellect, the heart or the life mind, but the inner soul which better knows the truth of its own destiny and mission."[38]

Bearing witness. The principal affirmation of Islam is not a statement of belief, although it often looks so externally. "The Muslim does *not* say, I believe that there is no god but God, and I believe that Muhammad is the apostle of God. Rather he asserts: 'I bear witness to' these facts."[39]

Faith is an assent and conscious acceptance that produces strong aspiration to realize fully that to which we assent. "In proportion as I have a sincerity and completeness of faith and an intensity of will to live according to that faith, I can become what it proposes to me."[40] Complete becoming bears complete witness. It is said that when twentieth-century Buddhist saint Dipa Ma bowed at the altar, it was as if the *Dhamma* was bowing to the *Dhamma*.[41]

A FINAL WORD

Any experiment requires wholehearted confident endeavor and always involves risk. Sometimes we feel the poignancy of that risk more than at other times. However, we have a refuge to which we can turn when spiritual living is difficult. "What then is the guiding light on which [we] can depend? The answer is *shraddha*, faith, will to believe, to live what [one] sees or thinks to be the truth of self and of existence."[42]

Chapter 12

FAITH IS SOMETIMES DIFFICULT

DOUBT, WAVERING, AND NOT-KNOWING

My doubt is terrible. Nothing can withstand it — it is a cursed hunger and I can swallow up every argument, every consolation and sedative.

— Søren Kierkegaard[1]

Faith, as anyone who has made a faith commitment knows, is not always easy. Often it feels uncertain or non-existent. This is painful to the extent that faith is important to a person. When faith is the heart of one's life, the pain can be agonizing. The playwright asked, "Can you think of anything worse one can do to anybody than take away their worship?"[2] Kierkegaard, quoted above, understood the anguish.

While some claim certainty about their religious positions, others find themselves plagued with doubt. Unfortunately, they often consider this a problem instead of recognizing it as an integral part of growth in faith. Sri Aurobindo pointed out that spiritual life offers much room to fall into misleading and often captivating error. There is some protection in "a certain amount of positive scepticism [and] a great caution and scrupulous intellectual rectitude."[3]

DYNAMICS OF DOUBT

Doubt, an honest process. Let us consult a poet about doubt:

> We have but faith: we cannot know
> For knowledge is of things we see ...
> You tell me Doubt is Devil-born ...
> There lives more faith in honest doubt,
> Believe me, than in half the creeds.[4]

Sometimes religion is presented in magical and fairy-tale beliefs. Some traditions also encourage childish, unquestioning acceptance. Since we must discard such immaturity, doubt is an important, integral part of faith's ripening. Mature faith cannot develop if we repress normal doubts and faith crises.[5] "An ever questioning attitude [may be] a modern way of keeping sacred things sacred."[6]

We all have some religious ideas that are not fully correct and perfect; we cannot see with the eye of God. Sri Aurobindo said, "Knowledge needs to be visited by doubt, otherwise [we] would remain obstinate in an ignorant belief and limited knowledge and unable to escape from [our] errors."[7] Theologian Paul Tillich said, "All these forms of insecurity and uncertainty belong to [our] essential finitude."[8] He also said that even Jesus had "doubt about his work — a doubt which breaks through most intensively on the Cross."[9]

Personal bases of doubt. Psychologist Gordon Allport said some doubting is helpful, and other reflects inferior motives.[10] Reactive doubting comes from traumatic events or unconscious processes. It occurs when an emotionally unsettling event cannot be integrated into a person's existing religious framework. We might doubt because we cannot believe that God could allow certain things to happen.

Habits of scientific thought and applying scientific criteria to religion lead some to doubt. Others resent not being able to test religious ideas as we test scientific hypotheses. Conflicting scientific and religious evidence sometimes causes trouble. Some people cannot adequately understand or accept metaphorical religious language; they apply tests of literalness to religious discourse. Some religious groups even encourage or insist upon such tests.

Other people have more self-serving reasons for doubting. They may doubt simply because faith no longer serves their personal advantage or desire. They might abandon faith to "get even with" their parents. Some people doubt because they are afraid of being duped. They do not want to let their own vague desires mislead them.

Doubt and the institution. Some people are troubled when they realize how historically conditioned any institution's understanding of God is. "There is always a danger of imagining a god with moral qualities like our own, vastly magnified and with the same blind spots."[11] Cultures create gods in their own image and offer such gods to the people. These gods prop up personal and group self-esteem, but such a mere projection can never be completely satisfying.

Very importantly, the failure of the religious institution itself is behind much doubt. People may see institutional religion as a dreary habit at best, and a real "con game" at worst. Such doubters do not feel that the church fires them into idealism. Some find the obvious hypocrisy in the church a problem. For others, changes in a tradition's practices and beliefs cause doubt. They need unchanging certainty about religious beliefs to be comfortable with faith.

Sometimes people leave a tradition for poor reasons. The egoistic nature may rebel against the yoke of restrictions that cramp it. According to Sri Aurobindo, "Even then it is often justified by some narrowness or imperfection of the *Shastra*[12] or by the degradation of the current rule of living into a merely restricting or lifeless convention."[13]

VARIETIES OF NOT-KNOWING

Agnosticism, atheism, and disbelief are quite different stances, and all differ from doubt. Still different is wavering uncertainty.

Agnosticism. Agnosticism — saying "I don't know" — is often quite paradoxical. It can be a very complex and respectful position. Many agnostics embrace an honesty lacking in some "true believers." Some agnostics realize that they can have only a very imperfect understanding of Ultimate Reality. They acknowledge this personal lack by not endorsing any necessarily limited positions.

One psychologist of religion defined five types of agnostics.[14] Some have no spiritual sense themselves but are reluctant to be dogmatic, realizing that other people do. A second group frankly admits to confusion about religious issues. The third type has more questions than answers and feels unprepared to draw conclusions.

Other agnostics are talented at speculating and may consider many religious understandings, but think it inappropriate to settle on just one. Still others have had experiential glimpses of spiritual reality, but realize how incomplete their understanding is. They do not want to foreclose judgment or to obscure what they have seen by covering it over with conceptual formulations. They know they have not seen all of truth, and do not want to make arrogant claims about what they *have* seen.

Unbelief. Western religion labels those who reject common notions with ugly words like "heretic" or "apostate." "The word 'unbeliever' implies a range of judgments from willful apostasy, stubborn rejection, or truculent opposition to sloth, lukewarmness. It is hard to use 'unbeliever' in a merely descriptive vein."[15]

Some people simply lack ability for the mutual trust necessary for relations with the divine. Other people seem to have no interest in their own contingent destiny.[16] Unbelief might also consist of balking at providence or having no sense of spiritual reality. All these unbelievers are not "against" anything, but are just not attuned to faith issues.

Some unbelief is not incompatible with faith. Disbelieving any particular idea does not necessarily mean rejecting the spiritual life. Psychologist Pruyser described some positive forms of unbelief. "Some unbelief is a rejection of childish propensities or an abandonment of natural wishes for protection and solace. This kind of unbelief requires self-scrutiny, intellectual honesty, and the courage of one's unpopular convictions."[17]

Religion promulgates authoritative doctrinal formulations that they hold to be beyond scrutiny. The required belief in these notions "is close to taboos. Some unbelief can be appreciated as a liberation of the mind from the fetters of taboo."[18] A Cistercian monk put it:

"Unless you lose your faith in God at least once a day, you are not growing spiritually."[19] Unless we are constantly willing to surrender current conceptual notions so that more mature ones can appear, we lock ourselves into a prison of stunted development.

Atheism. To adopt atheistic beliefs in the Western world is commonly a reactive choice. It often stems from pain inflicted by the religious establishment or the circumstances of life. Such atheism may itself become a militant belief stance. Some atheists have become trapped in the wrong questions discussed in chapter 1. Others defiantly adopt this stance when they cannot resolve some of the doubts discussed earlier in this chapter.

In some Eastern faiths, atheism is part of religious belief. Sometimes people perceive that God-concepts create more trouble than they resolve. They may opt to do spiritual practice to see for themselves, without previously adopting any notion about the Ultimate Reality. This stance is not a lack of faith, nor is it a rejection of any kind. It remains open to seeing and trusts that it *will* see.

Wavering and uncertainty. A quite troublesome condition is what Buddhists call "doubt." This is a motivational, rather than intellectual problem, so it is rather different from what we usually consider doubt. This wavering uncertainty cannot settle on anything long enough to investigate it sufficiently to determine its worth. If not overcome, wavering effectively closes down spiritual practice. Buddhists use the metaphor of a bee continually circling flowers, but not lighting on any. Unless the bee settles on one flower to draw nectar, it will never produce any honey.

Sri Aurobindo commented on this condition that can completely halt all spiritual endeavor. "Even a blind and ignorant faith is a better possession than the sceptical doubt which turns its back on our spiritual possibilities or the constant carping of the narrow [pettiness] which pursues our endeavor with a paralyzing incertitude."[20]

Doubt may settle on oneself, feeling that one is not capable of a proper response. It also may settle on teachings, teachers, the aim and goal of spiritual practice, or ultimate realities themselves. Laxity is its chief cause; wavering follows motivational halting. Renewed effort is the antidote. Such an understanding makes sense in light of William James's comments in chapter 10 on how faith becomes established.

REFINING THE BELIEFS IN FAITH

To the extent that our faith spawns particular religious beliefs, we must deal with them. We all seek cognitive clarity about what we do, so resorting to conceptual frameworks to articulate and understand our faith is common. Such activity calls for continual refinement.

Resolving doubt. Many problems of doubt come from making faith a rational exercise, trying to grasp with the intellect that which cannot be so grasped. Dag Hammarskjöld wrote movingly: "How many have been driven into outer darkness by empty talk about faith as something to be rationally comprehended, something 'true.' "[21] We can resolve such doubt by either accepting or rejecting a belief. We must willingly discard any understanding that ought to be surrendered.

We have first to understand that the intellect cannot be the ultimate guide in our search for spiritual truth — or, in itself, even an adequate one. "We have to reject paralyzing doubt or mere intellectual scepticism, [and] the seeking intelligence has to be trained to admit a certain large questioning [that is] not satisfied with half-truths."[22]

We must stay perfectly ready to move forward from truths already held and accepted to truths that are greater, corrective, completing, or transcending. The working faith of the intellect must not rest in superstitious, dogmatic, or limiting belief that gets attached to every temporary support or formula that comes our way. We must continually assent to the suggestions and guidance of the Spirit, saying a "yes" that effectively shapes how we live.

Holding beliefs. Recall psychologist Allport's "heuristic belief" (chapter 6). Such belief is "held tentatively until it can be confirmed or until it helps us discover a more valid belief."[23] This deeply religious psychologist meant that we affirm particular beliefs to help us better and more fully answer religious questions. However, we must continue to refine these beliefs as we develop deeper understanding. Mature faith requires ability to hold beliefs tentatively, always subject to revision.

Holding beliefs too rigidly brings unnecessary trauma and can be destructive to faith. "When [something] robs the notions hitherto bound up with faith of their solidity and unmistakable correspondence to faith, naturally a crisis erupts. But this is a crisis of belief, not faith. What begins as a crisis of belief turns into a crisis of faith, as a rule due to the intransigence of those who will tolerate no change because they do not distinguish between faith and belief."[24]

Critical tentativeness about religious beliefs can save our faith commitment from degenerating into fanaticism or bigotry.[25] Embracing tentativeness helps us go forward wholeheartedly without absolute certainty. It protects us from falling victim to the arrogance of our minds, which often like to believe that nothing is beyond their comprehension. We must willingly tolerate paradox and ambiguity.

One's own life and experience touch only a small part of the total meaning and value of life. We can appreciate the parts that other people have experienced and understand that they, too, are invested in values and truths that have helped them. Considering our own stance superior, simply because it is our stance, is just one more belief that we ought to evaluate.

Critically evaluating faith. Personality psychologist Allport held that full maturity requires a unifying philosophy of life that is sufficiently broad to integrate our entire life and give it meaning.[26] Although this need not be religious, religious philosophies usually are the most comprehensive. Allport said religion can cover "everything within experience and everything beyond experience under a unifying conception of the nature of all existence."[27]

Our religious beliefs must also be differentiated and integral, according to Allport. He explained these criteria. "Differentiation implies more than criticism; it implies an articulation and ordering of parts." We must also know our own attitudes "toward the chief phases of theoretical doctrine and the principal issues in the moral sphere, while at the same time maintaining a genuine sense of wholeness into which the articulated parts fit."[28]

To be integral faith must not shrink from dealing with the hard issues. A maturing faith must outgrow all childishness. We must get past seeing faith as a set of rules and beliefs and grasp its essence. A truly mature person cannot be content with "small" faith. When we critically evaluate our philosophy of life, we must be able to integrate it with other bodies of knowledge while not making it subservient to the demands of excessive rationality. A sufficiently broad religious framework of meaning can assimilate other knowledge.

ENDING NOTE

Intellectual knowledge is always mixed with falsehood and incompleteness. A point comes where we can no longer tolerate this, so "doubt and scepticism have their temporary uses [of] subjecting the truth itself to sceptical inquiry."[29] Deepening faith requires radical self-honesty and willingness to live with insecurity about beliefs. We must allow ourselves the creative activity of doubting. We must also not cling to particular beliefs.

The difficult places in faith can mature our faith. What may have seemed to be enemies of faith are revealed to be its friends. Defining faith as a choice to seek God avoids many of the problems we have discussed. Allport suggested we look at faith not as certain belief, but primarily as "aspirations, self-imposed ideals, approval of one way of life, the hoped-for completion of knowledge and the intended perfection of one's own nature."[30]

Chapter 13

FAITH IS A DARKNESS

EMBRACING THE UNKNOWN

Those who are into religion for comfort only clutter up the
doorstep.

— AUTHOR UNKNOWN[1]

Those who penetrate deeply into the life of faith eventually realize
how much faith is a darkness. Remaining faithful can be terrifying
at times. This chapter explores some reasons for this darkness and
what it requires of us.

CHOOSING RADICAL DARKNESS

Sometimes we must *choose* to embrace darkness. Bishop Robinson
said that Christian belief and practice require a new mold. We must
be prepared to surrender everything to be melted down — even
our most cherished religious categories and moral absolutes. The
first thing we must be ready to relinquish is our image of God.[2]
St. Clement said, "God is to be sought in darkness."[3]

Writing for people in a hurry to know God, John of the Cross
advocated radically stark nothingness in the life of faith. He taught
apparently drastic measures for us to enter the darkness that we must
eventually embrace to come to the Unknown. John wrote:

To come to the knowledge you have not
you must go by a way in which you know not.

116

> To come to the possession you have not
> you must go by a way in which you possess not.[4]

For those who like to feel grounded in religious knowledge, this method is painful. For those who want to possess God, it can be agony.

THE DARKNESS OF LIMITS

Knowing God in this life has three major limits. They are culture, language, and the nature of knowing God.

Of culture and nature. Faith is always embedded in a particular personality within a given culture. "Human faith has always, everywhere, been limited by psychological, sociological, and other contextual factors, by the knowledge and the temperament and the situation of the man or woman whose it is."[5]

Mahayana Buddhists distinguish between True Law in its supreme form and the empirical version of that Law, Law as it is taught. This latter is always subject to historical fluctuations.[6] A Christian writer said that the affirmation "I believe" is "the *conceptualization, culturally and historically conditioned,* of the Christian religious experience of belief in God."[7]

John of the Cross taught that deeply penetrating into the life of faith brings us to a point where all human faculties cease to serve us. "[God] leaves the intellect in darkness, the will in aridity, the memory in emptiness, and the affections in supreme affliction, bitterness, and anguish."[8] We are put into "emptiness and poverty of spirit and purged of every natural support, consolation, and apprehension, earthly and heavenly."[9]

Of language and concepts. Mystics and sages agree that "faith can never be expressed in words, neither in an aphorism nor in many volumes."[10] The *Kena Upanishad* says, "It is not understood by those who understand: it is understood by those who do not understand."[11] This is mirrored in the Bible's "I shall destroy the wisdom of the wise, and nullify the understanding of the understander" (1 Corinthians 1:19). Meister Eckhart even dared to say of Christian beliefs, "Everything that is said or written is in no way really so or true. Since God is inexpressible what we say [God] is is not in [God]."[12] Because words are our usual tool for understanding, this can leave us feeling like we have nothing to hold on to.

Sri Aurobindo realized how much we buck against accepting this. The philosophical mind wants to grasp God with its tools. Its business is to define and determine things for the finite intellect. "But the only way to determine the indeterminable is by some kind of universal negation, *neti neti.*"[13] Radhakrishnan echoed this teaching. "Once it enters the realm of human apprehension, [revelation] is subject to all the imperfections of the human mind. To claim finality or infallibility for human pictures of reality is to claim for [the human] what belongs to God."[14]

John of the Cross advised that we not cling to any particular ideas or opinions. We discern our experiences, but then relinquish them. We must not interpret or try to hold on to them. We must approach God not by knowledge, but by faith; not by knowing, but by unknowing, by letting go of the known. St. John said that the nature of both faith and the human intellect make faith necessarily a dark journey — all the way. Faith requires negation of opinion and understanding.[15]

In knowing God. Although we cannot grasp God conceptually, we can truly and directly know God. Our capacity to receive loving knowledge of God passively in the "substance of the soul" is virtually unlimited. St. John emphasized, however, that this knowing is experiential, not intellectual or conceptual. Once received, the communication of God can spill over into intellect, but not with conceptual clarity; "though faith brings certitude to the intellect, it does not produce clarity, but only darkness."[16] So even experiential knowledge of God does not bring conceptual clearness. It does not give us "distinct and particular knowledge [but] vague, dark, and general knowledge."[17]

THE DARKNESS OF FAITH

Voiding of understanding. Darkness is the only means for union with God since "faith nullifies the light of the intellect; and if this light is not darkened, the knowledge of faith is lost."[18] Because faith voids the intellect's understanding, causing darkness of reason, John of the Cross called the journey one of darkness. From beginning to end, we walk in faith, not in knowledge. No matter what confirming experiences we have, still the next step calls for more faith and moving further into darkness.

Sri Aurobindo noted that we seem caught between a double darkness — darkness and loss regarding worldly things and an even mightier darkness beyond. When we strive to know God utterly, we pass into a state that the mind cannot grasp in any way. At times it must negate all it knows of God for something beyond. We eventually find God again, seeming to transcend God, Godself. We find a greater Godhead by denying lesser understandings of God. Throughout this process, God also seems to hide; we see only appearances that we somehow know are other than God's true and eternal reality.[19]

"The night of the soul may be so black that faith may seem utterly to have left us."[20] But, through it all, the spirit within holds to faith, and we finally uncover new strength and assurance. After we experience such saving grace over and again, doubt eventually becomes impossible. While we are still in it, the blackness may even disable us at times. "Such disorder and incapacity are accepted by many great souls as a temporary passage or as the price to be paid for the entry into a wider existence."[21]

The burning desire. Sometimes our faith is intellectually very clouded and we are despondent in heart, wearied and exhausted by constant struggle. Even then, a deep inner desire for our goal still clings to faith and constantly answers its call.[22] Once we have truly accepted the summons of faith, this faith will remain firm deep inside and resist all attempts to defeat or slay it. But Sri Aurobindo cautioned, "It is not that the doubts of the intellect may not assail, the heart waver, the disappointed desire sink down exhausted on the wayside. That is almost inevitable at times."[23]

St. John called faith an obscure habit whose truths "transcend every natural light and infinitely exceed all human understanding."[24] By this habit we enjoy "divine and lofty knowledge."[25] This knowledge is not always consoling. God-seekers "suffer abandonment, supreme poverty, dryness. They find relief in nothing, nor does any thought console them, nor can they even raise the heart to God, so oppressed are they."[26] A burning desire, which keeps us oriented toward seeking its object, supports this habit of faith.[27] Faith burns within the heart, obscure and unclear, and impels our efforts to reach the good that God is, though we grasp it only dimly.

The transcendent goal. Traditions across time and space say that the Ultimate dwells in darkness. They teach that we come to God only through loss of sight and knowledge since God transcends these.[28] From Pseudo-Dionysius: "The Divine Darkness is the unapproachable light in which God is said to dwell."[29] St. Thomas Aquinas wrote: "The final attainment of [human] knowledge of God consists in knowing that we do not know [God], insofar as we realize that [God] transcends everything that we understand concerning [God]."[30]

The Chinese *Tao Te Ching* expresses this truth as "The name that can be named is not the Real Name."[31] Sri Aurobindo said that the "contradiction or non-existence of *Sachchidananda* is none other than *Sachchidananda* itself."[32] Mystic Plotinus wrote, "This is the soul's true goal, to touch that light and to behold it by means of that light itself, and not by any other light; even as we see not the sun by any light except its own."[33] The intellect simply cannot conceptually comprehend God.

LETTING GO

Faith's darkest times often signal the need to "let go." Letting go has many aspects. We must relinquish behaviors and attitudes contrary to faith. We must also surrender some favorite religious ideas, images, and idolatries. Other necessary relinquishments are often surprisingly painful. John of the Cross described "the extreme narrowness of the path, the denudation and freedom required of those who tread it."[34] Letting go can, indeed, be a living death.

Discarding a belief. Living with insecurity requires willingness to have particular beliefs disconfirmed. This reasonable humility recognizes that no one human being can possess total truth. We must know when it is time to let go of a belief that might once have served us well. A Sufi teacher said, "A particular belief serves as a vehicle for spiritual growth; when it ceases to stimulate growth, it needs to be released."[35] Sometimes we also must relinquish the tradition that offers the belief. When *any* relationship becomes destructive, divorce is sometimes the only solution.

We must work carefully and patiently wait for illumination when we purge religion of its problematic elements. Letting go out of frustration or annoyance that something is not working does not bring more luminosity. This "is not to purify but to pauperize."[36] The endeavor requires scrupulous self-honesty about our motives. Consultation with a spiritual teacher we trust and respect can be helpful.

Yielding self-image. Sometimes we must let go of our self-understandings. Spiritual growth requires that we see ourselves with an often painful honesty. When we have held ourselves to be good or virtuous in ways that are not so, we must revise self-opinion. Becoming able to laugh at our own foibles, self-inflation, and pretensions helps. Not seeing our own petty lacks as earth-shattering events puts them into proper perspective. It helps prevent unhelpful negative emotions. Those matured in faith have a clear picture of themselves, which they wear lightly.

For spiritual as well as personal health, our ego boundaries must extend to include others.[37] We must see their well-being as our own well-being. An Eastern teaching says that just as no sane person would let one hand cut off the other and harm the organism to which both belong, those who truly understand can inflict no harm on another being. Their self-identity has expanded into realizing that harming another harms the one organism of which both are a part.

Surrendering spiritual goods. We must also not be attached to our own spiritual work. "The faith in us must be free from attachment to the forms of our endeavor and the successive stages of our realization."[38] We go through various steps that are sequentially helpful. What may seem at one time to be spiritual finalities, we later realize were just steps of transition. We must withdraw the working faith that supported them in favor of greater wisdom and fuller understanding.

Some mystics have suggested that the final transformation in spiritual seeking might even mean relinquishing affiliation with any given tradition — or even with religion itself. "One could thus ask whether religious development can proceed to the point at which it eliminates itself or becomes something else."[39] This may be, perhaps, a sense of world citizenship spiritually, of seeing all other persons of ripening faith as one's spiritual family.

Giving up control. True spiritual surrender means giving up being in charge. This spiritual truth is heralded from the oldest time-honored traditions to contemporary Twelve Step programs. Surrender makes us feel insecure until it is wholehearted and its fruits start to be seen. Yet "to flee from insecurity is to miss the point of being human."[40] The great religious prophets lived in insecurity, but their followers often make feeling safe their highest priority. Security-seeking can distort truth and make impossible the deeper understandings of a tried and tested faith.

From his Nazi prison cell, theologian Dietrich Bonhoeffer said that mature religiousness requires that we live in the world without the comfort of religious certainty. He said, "The God who makes us live in this world without using [God] as a working hypothesis is the God before whom we are ever standing. Before God and with [God] we live without God."[41]

At periods in our spiritual work when we feel totally bereft, we must willingly wait for deliverance. "At one stage it becomes necessary to refuse to accept [anything] as definite and final and to hold it in a questioning suspension until it is given its right place and luminous shape of truth in a spiritual experience."[42]

TOWARD FULFILLMENT

Many great traditions say that we have to arrive at a perfectly surrendered balance and equanimity to come to fruition in our search for God. The darkness brings us to this. A Buddhist writer taught that, when one fully understands the nature of things, one "no longer clings to anything and is filled with perfect equanimity regarding all formations."[43] John of the Cross said: "Not finding satisfaction in anything or understanding anything in particular, and remaining in its emptiness and darkness [the soul] embraces all things with great preparedness."[44] In this state we are most open to God. We are most apt to be graced when we are the most empty.

Chapter 14

FAITH IS A DYNAMIC PROCESS

COMING HOME TO GOD

When the realization comes, the faith divinely fulfilled and completed will be transformed into an eternal flame of knowledge.

— SRI AUROBINDO[1]

And now our last topic on faith — faith as a dynamic process. A commentator on the *Yoga Sutras* of Patanjali said faith means having the heart "pleasantly inclined towards attaining yoga" (union with God).[2] When the Buddha was asked, "What wealth is best to have?" he replied: "Faith is the wealth here best to have. By faith the flood is crossed."[3]

The West often sees faith as some inscrutable "thing" that we either mysteriously have or do not have. In discussing faith as choice, darkness, and experiment, we questioned this idea. Now we look at faith developmentally — at different stages of the active, growing process that constitutes a living faith. We look at faith as bringing us home, crossing the flood, leading us to union with God.

THE BUDDHIST "AWAKENING OF FAITH"

An early Mahayana Buddhist text very clearly stated that purely verbal or conceptual faith — words without works — is not genuine faith. Faith is an active process. Asvaghosha's treatise *The Awakening of Faith in the Great Source of All* described various ways of spiritual progress.[4] We will look at two of them.

Perfection of faith. One way faith develops is through the perfection of faith itself. We know that faith is being perfected when three changes occur. First: we more and more rightly comprehend the Ultimate Reality. Most often, we cannot conceptualize this intuitive knowledge in any way. Second: we more and more understand virtue and take increasing joy in practicing goodness. Finally: we come to greater love and compassion, which seek to help all beings be delivered from all kinds of suffering.

Practice of virtues. Another way of growth is by practicing virtues that constitute the very basis of a living faith. We undertake giving or generosity by realizing that there is no withholding in the divine and that we conform to divine law by not withholding. Aware that there is no immorality in the divine, we practice morality and purity.

Knowing that in the divine there is no impatience but only serenity, we practice patience. Through all life's vicissitudes — pleasure or pain, praise or blame, gain or loss, isolation or companionship — we remain calm and accepting. We do not try to avoid the unpleasant or cling to what is pleasant.

Realizing that there is no indolence in the divine, we practice endurance. We have unfailing zeal for kind actions and energetic spiritual practice for the good of all. Finally, since there is no darkness, confusion, or ignorance in the divine, we practice meditation to discipline the mind and attain penetrating wisdom.

WESTERN PSYCHOLOGICAL MODEL

James Fowler's Western perspective on faith development emphasizes concepts and ideas far more than Eastern models.[5] Fowler does, however, define his stages according to *how* we stand *in* faith, rather than on the contents *of* faith.

Transitions. We can see each stage as a milepost that we gradually approach and leave. Being established in any stage is comfortable, and upsetting the equilibrium to move on is painful. Fowler said he encounters many eleven-year-old "atheists" who cannot move from childish to more adolescent faith. Going beyond the faith of adolescence is even more uncomfortable and costly.

Primal faith. Fowler's first stage is primal faith. Our early relationships with self, world, and nurturers during infancy leave us feeling that the world is basically either good or bad. These experiences shape later understandings and images of God.

Intuitive-projective faith. When we develop language, around age two, fantasies, stories, and images start to shape faith. Imagination tries to make sense of the world, and we adopt the faith symbols of those around us. This faith is very egocentric. Gordon Allport tells about little Tommy taken to church for the first time by his mother. Seeing the cross on the steeple, he cried out, "Look, Mommy, a T for Tommy." Allport said that Tommy has yet to understand that this symbol means crossing out the "I."[6]

Mythic-literal faith. Around school age, mythic-literal faith can emerge. We then rely on the rules, stories, and implicit values of our community. Faith is very concrete and literal with neither reflection on nor understanding of inner experience. Some adults never outgrow such unexamined self-identification with the faith community's stories. Such faith is very common among adolescents who remain religious.

Synthetic-conventional. At about the time of early adolescence, synthetic-conventional faith becomes possible. Such faith supports and holds together our sense of self and life. Emerging self-consciousness, aware that its self-images do not form a coherent whole, tries to unify the various elements of life within a faith perspective. We often hold such faith with great intensity and do not objectify it for critical reflection.

This stage's unifying faith synthesis is not a unique or personal creation, but comes from other people. It is conventional in the fullest sense of the word, dependent on the conventions of those around us. Many people establish their entire faith equilibrium in this stage and go through their whole lives with an essentially unexamined set of values and beliefs.

Individuative-reflexive faith. To move to individuative-reflexive faith, we must objectify, examine, and make crucial choices about both our personal and current faith identities. We must thoroughly review everything that is tacit and unexamined. We must freely commit to some path and be accountable for the choice.

Fowler holds that the early twenties is usually the youngest we can do this. For some this growth comes with even more pain in their thirties and forties, and for others it never comes. Genuine choice means we might choose against what we have already practiced. It carries the risk that we will not be able to find a choice with which we can be comfortable. We then lose earlier security and have nothing with which to replace it.

Conjunctive, or paradoxical-consolidative faith. To attain conjunctive faith, which is usually not possible before mid-life, we must realize that truth is far more complex than we earlier believed. We must recognize that we *have* chosen and *are* choosing and that we could make other choices with equal justification or lack thereof.

Such faith combines commitment to personal values with deep respect for others' choices. Our loyalty is to a community of communities; this makes uncritical devotion, rigid beliefs, holy wars, and self-righteousness alien notions. This high stage of faith manifests great tolerance.

Conjunctive faith must acknowledge realities that earlier faith could avoid or deny. It commonly brings tension between experienced polarities of life and humble awareness of personal lack and need for true self-knowledge. It requires acceptance of a cosmic loneliness and awareness that some things are not possible. Death and aging become realities with which one must deal. Living in conjunctive faith is being in but not of the world and can be very uncomfortable.

Universalizing faith. Two steps are necessary for universalizing faith, Fowler's last stage. We must "decentrate" from ourselves and view the world through the eyes and experiences of the collective, including those quite different from ourselves. Our values then come from this universal perspective. We also must not prefer the persons, tradition, culture, and other trappings with particular ties to ourselves. This amounts to radical self-emptying, to selflessness that any tradition would recognize as sainthood. Fowler considers this stage very rare; it is the stance of religious geniuses.

THREE STAGES OF FAITH

The Theravadan Buddhist tradition defines three broad types of faith. They occur successively, so we also can see them as stages of faith.

Bright faith. Bright faith arises when a particular teaching attracts us. Perhaps the teaching itself has strong appeal. It may be the path of someone whose life seems quite beautiful. Something about the teaching may be associated with a highly positive experience — such as peace, beauty, or goodness. For whatever reason, we see a particular teaching as worthy and decide to try it. The principal function of bright faith is to get us to do spiritual practice.

Bright faith, however, is always doomed to fade. It is rather like the first flush of romantic love; if something of greater substance does not follow, bright faith slips away. We are left wondering what we ever found attractive in the first place. Even the most beautiful life has some discordant note. The most appealing teaching has parts that are harder to accept. Faith based only on initial attraction will eventually die.

Confirmed faith. If we respond to bright faith by practicing a worthy teaching, another kind of faith starts to grow. Our lives noticeably improve, and this confirms our faith. We tasted and found it "sweet" (Psalm 34:8); we subjected the teaching to tests that it passed. This does not mean that acting on faith is always pleasant but that the teaching produces the results it promises.

Confirmed faith is stronger and can endure some hard times; we can stand being tried. Faith is not yet entirely secure, however. Should we become lax, confirmed faith may start to wane when we face other satisfactions antagonistic to faith's demands.

Invincible faith. Eventually faith becomes invincible, the third stage. Even when it feels like faith is uncertain, we still hold to the course we have set ourselves — no turning back. This does not mean that we become cognitively certain of particular opinions; such is foreign to the Buddhist understanding of faith, which is a matter of the heart. The heart simply becomes fully established in spiritual practice. From the Buddha: "When one knows the defilements of the mind and gets rid of them, one becomes possessed of unwavering confidence in the Buddha, in *Dhamma*.[7]

A good example of invincible faith, which could not hold any opinions with certainty, is Carmelite nun Thérèse of Lisieux.[8] While painfully dying at a young age, she also suffered terribly from loss of the sense of God and heaven. The suffering was probably made worse by a Christian education that said she *should* feel certain about these ideas. Yet behind the loss of certainty about spiritual reality, Thérèse's faith held her in deep commitment to spiritual practice. She faithfully endured intense physical and mental anguish and then died in ecstasy.

THE END OF FAITH

Believing and seeing. For St. John of the Cross, faith is God's communication, which grasps its object — God — securely. Faith is both the way to God and the possession of God. "The likeness between faith and God is so close that no other difference exists than that between [setting one's heart on] God and seeing [God]. The greater one's faith the closer is one's union with God."[9] Faith grasps God as God is; later our experience confirms the reality we sought. Faith, though certain in its grasp of God, does *not* involve clear understanding.

Faith requires active commitment. John said that although it excludes intellectual clarity and certainty, it must include charity.[10] Faith weakens if we do not make vigorous effort toward self-purification. Committed living in faith increasingly opens us to God's self-communication in the "substance of the soul"; God flows into and fills our capacity to know God. As we grow in faith, increasingly only God resides in our hearts. We know with God's knowing and love with God's loving. In this life, however, the vision of God is not distinct; faith remains dark.

Support from above. Sri Aurobindo taught that, even when a tradition is still the best rule for the human average, some spiritually developed people are better off not being bound by it. They are called to go beyond "to a more absolute perfection; [they] must learn to live in the liberty of the Spirit."[11]

Sri Aurobindo claimed that all who faithfully follow a suitable path will come to their heart's desire, to the spiritual realization for which each is suited. He cited Krishna's promise in the *Bhagavad Gita*: "Whatever form of Me any devotee with faith desires to worship, I make that faith firm and undeviating."[12]

"Faith is a support from above; it is the brilliant shadow thrown by a secret light that exceeds the intellect and its data; it is the heart of a hidden knowledge that is not at the mercy of immediate appearances. At the end, the flickering of faith will cease; for we shall see his face and feel always the Divine Presence."[13] Ultimately, this support brings us home.

Fruits of faith. A disciple of the Buddha said that after continuous striving in faith, working hard at spiritual practice, one finally becomes convinced: "These teachings which before I had only heard, I now dwell in their personal experience, and having penetrated them with wisdom, I now see them." The Buddha replied, "Well said, well said."[14] This seeing is our task; it is our goal and our fruition.

Our faith is more and more justified as we come to higher knowledge and love of God. We start to see many great and small significances that previously escaped our limited mentality. As faith passes into knowledge, we see beyond any doubt that all happens within the working of a great wisdom. In the highest state, our whole being is faith. "We feel the presence of the *Ishwara*[15] and feel all our existence and consciousness and thought and will and action in [God's] hand and consent [completely] to the direct and immanent and occupying will of the Spirit."[16]

SUMMARY

Sri Aurobindo said, "It is by an inmost will to live [the Divine] or be it that we come by it; but this does not mean that it does not already exist beyond us."[17] God *is* before we come to God; God's being does not depend on our effort. Sri Aurobindo simply summarized this process of coming to God. At the beginning of spiritual life, we must make our own effort. Then both God and we work together.

Finally, God does it all. Then in the end we realize that all along it was all done by God.

"Only through the self-knowledge we gain by pursuing the fleeting light in the depth of our being do we reach the point where we can grasp what faith is."[18] As we pursue the light and are willing to see, we see more and more. We choose faith. Faith then tries and tests us in fire and beats us into the form of faithful people. As Augustine said, "I embrace faith, in order to understand; and I understand, the better to embrace faith."[19] In the end, we *see*, we *taste*, we *know* that which we sought in the flickering light. Blessed become those who hold themselves constant through even the hardest times!

POSTSCRIPT

Wilfred Cantwell Smith argued, "The identifying of faith with belief led many in the Church to urge that it was important to say 'yes' to the belief question, and many critical thinkers to hold that it was important to say 'no' to the faith question. Both were wrong."[1] I hope by now you would agree with him.

LEVELS OF KNOWING

While we can agree that faith is a kind of knowledge, a knowing of spiritual truths, we must understand what we mean. A summary of different ways of knowing will help.

A Buddhist understanding. A Tibetan Buddhist lama delineated three degrees of knowledge to which we might aspire. The first comes from opinions to which desires and simple sense impressions lead us. Such knowledge is often full of error. However, this wishful thinking constitutes the faith of some people. Next comes scientific knowledge, as usually understood, applying reasoning and other methodologies to the first level of knowledge. Here we have a faith that depends on concepts and cognitive operations, on argumentation and theologizing. Finally, the highest degree of knowledge lies beyond reason. This intuitive state of consciousness, in which reality is realized free from any dualities and partialities, is a fruit of meditation.[2]

Types of knowledge. A similar framework speaks of four types of knowledge. The first is that received on the word of another. Unless we verify such knowledge for ourselves, it remains only hearsay. The second comes from study and reflection about what we have heard.

This can bring greater understanding. A still deeper learning comes from what life itself teaches us. For this reason, some cultures honor the elderly simply because they have had more time to acquire such wisdom. Finally, the deepest knowing comes from meditation experience; this knowing is life-transforming. Hindu Vedanta discusses the first, second, and fourth of these ways to know.[3]

Christian philosopher and theologian Jacques Maritain also distinguished different types of knowledge. He differentiated between the knowledge that meditation and mysticism give and those kinds that derive from the intellect.[4]

AN INTERFAITH REFLECTION

I ask you what I once asked myself: what value is a faith that one must constantly treat like a hothouse flower? A hothouse flower that we must continually protect from any notions that may challenge it in any way? The payoff for openness to truth wherever we find it is faith settled on a much firmer ground than the limited understandings of just one perspective or tradition. That very open-mindedness makes faith stronger, even invincible.

Religious similarities. Some people are disturbed by the similarities in the myths surrounding incarnations of God. Some are even upset by the similarities in spiritual teachings found across the traditions. For me, these correspondences greatly strengthen faith. God is so much bigger than we were first taught; God is big enough to manifest to different cultures as needed.

Most Christians look for the second coming of Jesus — of the glorified Christ, the Word of God. Those who can accept the divine promises made in Eastern traditions may say that Jesus *has* already come again — probably more than once. Most people did not recognize him because they insisted he come in the only form they were willing to consider true.

Followers of two contemporary Indian women — known popularly as Ammaji and Mother Meera — consider them to be incarnations of the Divine Mother aspect of God. I have not met either woman, but people I know and respect have. Of Ammaji, devotees say that when you look into her eyes you see no separate, distinct person; you see only unfathomable love. In her presence you feel bathed in her tender care. Of Mother Meera, I was told that being in her presence opens you to awareness of the hidden corners of your soul. Her being forces upon you needed self-knowledge and the will to do something about it.

I am not saying that these women are divine incarnations. I can only say what any honest person would have to say: Who can really know what and who these women are? We know they have led many people to God; they produce good fruits. We know also that they allow others to consider them *avatars*. To "write them off" without any consideration would speak poorly of anybody's faith.

Celebrating diversity. An Eastern saying recommends that we seek what the religious giants sought rather than lock ourselves into the boxes that their earlier followers built. Rupturing divisive boundaries — those that declare all other stances to be less true or good than our own — seems a necessary step in today's world. We can then appreciate the various ways in which people seek the Ultimate Reality. We can respect and encourage all those on any proven path, accepting its validity as we want our own way accepted.

If we stop comparing ourselves with others, we do not have to consider them wrong for us to be right. We can appreciate religious diversity as different expressions of the one Reality on whose image all is patterned. We can glory in this diversity as a beautiful jewel seen from many different angles to show the full range of its opulence. We can see our diversity as different petals on the same flower or different leaves on the same tree — all basically very much alike, but each with its slightly different features, and all part of one organism. We can exult in the magnificent kaleidoscope of Reality, the same basic materials showing different patterns with every slight turn of perspective. And we can learn from each other, appreciating the unique gifts that each tradition offers.

MY "OVERBELIEF"

The great William James ended his classic, *The Varieties of Religious Experience*, with a personal *apologia*. Acknowledging that it went beyond objectively provable data, he called it his "overbelief." It seems appropriate that one writing a book on faith offer a similar statement. Here is the short, simplified version.

I believe that "God is one" (Deuteronomy 6:4; Mark 12:29), not that there is *one* God, which makes God an object among other objects. I believe that seekers across history have known God in the various traditions, under different guises, by different names, and at different degrees of depth. I believe that we also can know God in various ways and that doing so enriches us. I believe that the more deeply we experience God, the more we see the oneness of all that exists in the cosmos. We see that all are one in all, and all are one in God (John 16:21).

I believe that God has come to us in various cultures at different times and will continue to do so as we need it.[5] I believe that some of these visitations have enfleshed the fullness of divinity, while some can be considered partial incarnations. I believe that all these forms are also culturally conditioned and become subject to the encroaching of human error in the way they are offered to people. I believe that traditions built on these forms need constant renewal. I believe that God-seekers must search for forms appropriate and helpful to them and not let fear, authority, or conformity prevent them from doing so.

I believe that God guides our growth back toward God. I believe also that we must make our own effort in spiritual work. I believe that if we but do our part, God's gracious gift will make up for our deficiencies and surely guide us home. I believe that sincerity, commitment, aspiration, surrender, and wholeheartedness — rather than the specific form within which one works — draw that grace. However, I also believe that we must exercise great discretion in choosing the forms in which we seek God so that we are not led astray by whim, superficial glitter, or habit.

I believe that the true spiritual community of seekers cuts across the conventional lines of traditions. I believe that church — the gathering of the people — is defined by the extent to which one cares about spiritual issues, not by the accidents of birth, geography, or socialization. I believe that we all, if we do but care and act on that care, will come home to the oneness of God and of all being. Finally, I believe that this formulation of my faith can, must, and will need revision.

MY WISH

My wish for the reader is that he or she come to a very vast, spiritually enhancing openness. I wish for all that faith come to be much more broadly defined than the narrower ways taught most of us when we were young. The world no longer has time for such distrust and divisiveness. May your faith be released from whatever hothouses it inhabits and come to blossom fully in the lushness of the wider universe of God's truth.

NOTES

Preface

1. Raimundo Panikkar, *The Intrareligious Dialogue* (New York: Paulist Press, 1978), 7.

2. *Gentling the Heart: Buddhist Loving-Kindness Practice for Christians* (New York: Crossroad, 1994) is dedicated to Joseph Goldstein, my principal Buddhist teacher. This book also acknowledges other Buddhist teachers with whom I have practiced, especially Theravadan Buddhist monks in the Burmese Mahasi tradition.

3. We lead "Silence and Awareness" retreats together, which are the basis for our book *Purifying the Heart: Buddhist Insight Meditation for Christians* (New York: Crossroad, 1994).

Chapter 1: The Wrong Questions

1. J. B. Phillips, *Your God Is Too Small* (New York: Macmillan Company, 1953).

2. Carl Gustav Jung, *Memories, Dreams, Reflections* (New York: Random House Vintage Books, 1965).

3. John of the Cross, *The Ascent of Mount Carmel* II, 4:4, in *The Collected Works of St. John of the Cross*, rev. ed., trans. Kieran Kavanaugh and Otilio Rodriguez (Washington, D.C.: Institute of Carmelite Studies, 1991).

4. Thomas Aquinas, *Summa Theologica* II-II, 1, 2, *ad* 2.

5. Phillips, *Your God Is Too Small*, Table of Contents.

6. Ibid., vi.

7. Article no. 168, p. 46. I have not purchased this book, nor will I. I take the deliberate choice of sexist language as a sign that it was not written for women. My friend and colleague Fr. Kevin Culligan gave me access to his copy to get the information I wanted.

8. Abraham Maslow, *Religions, Values, and Peak Experiences* (Columbus: Ohio State University Press, 1964), 21.

9. Sarvepalli Radhakrishnan, *Recovery of Faith: The Way toward a Religion of the Spirit* (New York: Harper & Brothers, 1955), 29.

10. Article no. 156, p. 42.

11. My favorite Buddhist prophecy, told me by Joseph Goldstein of Insight Meditation Society, is a medieval Tibetan one. It states that when horses have wheels and the iron bird flies in the sky, the saving teachings of the Buddha will come to the land of the red man. How confusing this vision, so transparent to modern America, must have been to the medieval Tibetan who faithfully reported it! And, of course, the Buddha's teachings have exploded into the United States in the late twentieth century.

12. Phillips, *Your God Is Too Small*, 38.

13. For a striking exposition of this theme, see Michael Crosby, *The Dysfunctional Church: Addiction and Codependency in the Family of Catholicism* (Notre Dame, Ind.: Ave Maria Press, 1991).

14. We find most of this in Matthew 23.

15. Swami Prabhavananda, *The Spiritual Heritage of India: A Clear Summary of Indian Philosophy and Religion* (Hollywood, Calif.: Vedanta Press, 1979), 20.

16. As Buddhists use the very rich Sanskrit word *Dharma* (*Dhamma* in the Buddha's Pali language) it means eternal law, Truth, the path, Reality, the foundation of all realities, the way, the pattern underlying all that is real, that which supports and upholds us, that which leads us home, the teachings, and so on. Similarities to the Christian *Logos*, or Word of God, as well as the Holy Spirit are obvious.

17. *Majjhima-nikaya* I, 479–80. (*Kitagiri Sutta*).

18. Prabhavananda, *The Spiritual Heritage of India*, 227.

19. Religious symbols and language will be discussed thoroughly in chapter 3.

20. Maslow, *Religions, Values, and Peak Experiences*, 21.

21. Raimundo Panikkar, *The Intrareligious Dialogue* (New York: Paulist Press, 1978), 18–19.

22. Wilfred Cantwell Smith, "The Death of God," in *Questions of Religious Truth* (New York: Charles Scribner's Sons, 1967), 16.

23. Ibid.

24. Sri Aurobindo Ghose, *The Human Cycle, The Ideal of Human Unity, War and Self-Determination* (Pondicherry, India: Sri Aurobindo Ashram, 1971), 125.

Chapter 2: Concepts and Reality

1. Leslie Dewart, *The Future of Belief: Theism in a World Come of Age* (New York: Herder & Herder, 1966), 167–68.

2. G. W. Allen, *William James* (New York: Viking Press, 1967), 415.

3. Sri Aurobindo Ghose. I copied this quote directly from the writings of Sri Aurobindo at the Sri Aurobindo Ashram in Pondicherry, India. Unfortu-

nately, I did not also copy the specific source and I have been unable to locate it in books available to me.

4. William James, *The Varieties of Religious Experience* (New York: McKay, 1902), cited from Collier Book edition (1961), 349.

5. For a discussion of this, see Paul Pruyser, *Between Belief and Unbelief* (New York: Harper & Row, 1974), 259.

6. Ibid., 258.

7. Published as Mary Jo Meadow and Kevin Culligan, "Congruent Spiritual Paths: Christian Carmelite and Theravadan Buddhist Vipassana," *Journal of Transpersonal Psychology* 19 (1987): 181–96.

8. My teacher was Joseph Goldstein, at Insight Meditation Society, Barre, Mass., October 1985.

9. See note 16 in chapter 1 for explanation of the word *Dhamma*.

10. To understand how psychologists view attribution theory, see Kelly Shaver, *An Introduction to Attribution Processes* (Cambridge, Mass.: Winthrop, 1975).

11. This is a common axiom throughout the writings of Sri Aurobindo which is summed up in *The Synthesis of Yoga* (Pondicherry, India: Sri Aurobindo Ashram, 1976).

12. For a detailed discussion of the processes by which we handle the threat of disconfirmation of important beliefs, see Leon Festinger, Henry W. Riecken, and Stanley Schachter, *When Prophecy Fails: A Social and Psychological Study of a Modern Group That Predicted the Destruction of the World* (New York: Harper Torchbooks, 1956).

13. Sri Aurobindo, *The Ideal of Human Unity, War and Self-Determination* (Pondicherry, India: Sri Aurobindo Ashram, 1971), 97.

14. Wilfred Cantwell Smith, *Faith and Belief* (Princeton, N.J.: Princeton University Press, 1979), 76. I rely heavily on him for understanding the changes in meaning of faith-related words.

15. Ibid., 85. In the Bible, see James 2:19–20.

16. Ibid., 118.

17. Ibid., 105.

18. Ibid., 113.

19. St. John's teachings on concepts and faith are mainly in Book II of *The Ascent of Mount Carmel*, in *The Collected Works of St. John of the Cross*, rev. ed., trans. Kieran Kavanaugh and Otilio Rodriguez (Washington, D.C.: Institute of Carmelite Studies, 1991).

20. Abhishiktananda (Henri Le Saux), *Saccidananda: A Christian Approach to Advaitic Experience* (Delhi, India: ISPCK, 1984), 10.

Chapter 3: Symbol, Ritual, Myth, Metaphor

1. Samuel Langhorne Clemens, *Mark Twain's Notebook, Prepared for Publication with Comments* by Albert Bigelow Paine (New York: Harpers, 1935), 237.

2. From the television comedy, *All in the Family.*

3. Abhishiktananda (Henri Le Saux), *Saccidananda: A Christian Approach to Advaitic Experience* (Delhi, India: ISPCK, 1984), 201.

4. Carl Gustav Jung, *Memories, Dreams, Reflections* (New York: Random House Vintage Books, 1965).

5. Erich Fromm, *The Forgotten Language* (New York: Holt, Rinehart, & Winston, 1951).

6. Article no. 170, p. 46.

7. Sri Aurobindo Ghose, *The Life Divine* (Pondicherry, India: Sri Aurobindo Ashram, 1973), I, 69.

8. G. Clarke, "The Need for New Myths," *Time*, January 17, 1972, 50.

9. Erich Fromm, *Psychoanalysis and Religion* (New Haven: Yale University Press, 1950), 103.

10. Ibid., 105.

11. On Ted Koppel's *Nightline* show during January 1994.

12. Paul Pruyser, *A Dynamic Psychology of Religion* (New York: Harper & Row, 1968), 94.

13. Ibid., 92. Minor deletions not indicated.

14. John of the Cross, *Ascent of Mount Carmel* II, 19:5, in *The Collected Works of St. John of the Cross*, rev. ed., trans. Kieran Kavanaugh and Otilio Rodriguez (Washington, D.C.: Institute of Carmelite Studies, 1991). Minor deletions not indicated.

15. Abraham Maslow, *Religions, Values, and Peak Experiences* (Columbus: Ohio State University Press, 1964).

16. Sri Aurobindo, *The Human Cycle, The Ideal of Human Unity, War and Self-Determination* (Pondicherry, India: Sri Aurobindo Ashram, 1971), 125.

17. Richard A. Hunt, "Mythological-Symbolic Religious Commitment: The LAM Scales," *Journal for the Scientific Study of Religion* 11 (1972): 43.

18. Sri Aurobindo, *The Synthesis of Yoga* (Pondicherry, India: Sri Aurobindo Ashram, 1976), 746.

19. Wilfred Cantwell Smith, *Faith and Belief* (Princeton, N.J.: Princeton University Press, 1979), 66. Minor deletions not indicated.

Chapter 4: Faith's Places of Refuge

1. Eugene C. Kennedy, *Believing: The Nature of Belief and Its Role in Our Lives* (Garden City, N.Y.: Doubleday, 1974), 208.

2. See *Bhayabherava Sutta* (*Majjhima Nikaya* 4) v. 35, for one of many statements of taking refuge in the Buddha, Dhamma, and Sangha.

3. An *avatar* is an incarnation of the Divine. It is a human being who incorporates the fullness of divinity, come to be among us to guide, teach, save, and help us.

4. When I mentioned my opinion about this to my good friend Carmelite friar Daniel Chowning, he brought me a quote from theologian Edward Schillebeeckx — which we have been unable to locate again — saying essentially the same thing.

5. Sarvepalli Radhakrishnan, *Recovery of Faith: The Way toward a Religion of the Spirit* (New York: Harper & Brothers, 1955), 159.

6. Sri Aurobindo Ghose, *Essays on the Gita* (Pondicherry, India: Sri Aurobindo Ashram Trust, 1972), chap. 15.

7. *Bhagavad-Gita*, IV:8. The *Gita* seems clearly the most loved scripture of Hindus. Believed by some to have been interpolated at a later date, it is part of the great epic *The Mahabharata*. In the *Gita* Krishna, an incarnation of Vishnu, the second person of a Hindu trinity, teaches his disciple Arjuna. Many passages read much like the Last Supper Discourse in the Gospel of John. This scripture is available in many translations and editions.

8. *Sad-dharma pundarika*, IV.

9. *Bhagavad-Gita*, IX:18.

10. *Majjhima Nikaya* 1, 190–91; *Samyutta-nikaya* III, 120; *Khandha Samyutta* xxii.87.7. The word *Dhamma* (or *Dharma*) is fully explained in note 16, chapter 1.

11. See John 1:1–2.

12. Walter Wink, professor of biblical interpretation at Auburn Theological Seminary in New York City, in "Faith, Intellect Meet in Jesus Studies," *Minneapolis Star Tribune*, August 1, 1994, 4A.

13. Marcus Borg, head of the Jesus Seminar and professor of religion and culture at Oregon State University, in "Faith, Intellect Meet in Jesus Studies," *Minneapolis Star Tribune*, August 1, 1994, 4A.

14. These writings are available. See *Hermetica: The Ancient Greek and Latin Writings Which Contain Religious or Philosophic Teachings Ascribed to Hermes Trismegistus*, vol. 1: *Introduction, Texts, and Translation*, ed. and trans. Walter Scott (Boston: Shambhala, 1985).

15. Seiichi Yagi and Leonard Swidler, *A Bridge to Buddhist-Christian Dialogue* (New York: Paulist Press, 1990), 15.

16. Sri Aurobindo, *The Human Cycle, The Ideal of Human Unity, War and Self-Determination* (Pondicherry, India: Sri Aurobindo Ashram, 1971), 211.

17. You can read about this in the Bible in the Acts of the Apostles.

18. Theodore Hesburgh of the University of Notre Dame, in Eugene C. Kennedy, *Believing*, 95.

19. Hobart Mowrer, *The Crisis in Psychiatry and Religion* (New York: Van Nostrand Reinhold, 1961); *The New Group Therapy* (New York: Van Nostrand Reinhold, 1964).

20. *Mahaparinibbana Sutta* 2:26.
21. *Rohitassa Sutta, Samyutta Nikaya,* i, 62.
22. *Vinaya-pitaka* I, 302.
23. Sri Aurobindo, *The Human Cycle,* 122.

Chapter 5: Faith Is Not What You Believe

1. Wilfred Cantwell Smith, *Faith and Belief* (Princeton, N.J.: Princeton University Press, 1979), 127.
2. For more on the words "believe," "belief," and "faith," see above pp. 13–14 and 33.
3. Smith, *Faith and Belief,* 77.
4. Abhishiktananda (Henri Le Saux), *The Farther Shore* (Delhi, India: ISPCK, 1975), 60.
5. This was said many times in many different ways by the Buddha. The major source is *Kesaputtiya Sutta,* A. 1., 188, the sermon to the Kalamas.
6. The *Qur'an* (often written "Koran" in English) is the sacred book of Islam. Its status for Muslims corresponds to that of the person of Jesus in Christianity.
7. Smith, *Faith and Belief* discusses this on p. 39.
8. Ibid., 45.
9. *Canki Sutta.*
10. Sri Aurobindo Ghose, *The Human Cycle, The Ideal of Human Unity, War and Self-Determination* (Pondicherry, India: Sri Aurobindo Ashram, 1971), 123.
11. Sigmund Freud, *The Future of an Illusion* (1927), trans. W. D. Robson-Scott (Garden City, N.Y.: Doubleday Anchor, 1961), 47.
12. *Kesaputtiya Sutta,* A., i., 188, sermon to the Kalamas.
13. See especially Matthew 23:13–36.
14. Swami Vivekananda, *Complete Works of Vivekananda* (Mayavati, India: Advaita Ashrama, 1932), 4: 182–83.
15. William James, *The Varieties of Religious Experience* (New York: McKay, 1902), cited from Collier Books edition (1961), 349.
16. Sri Aurobindo, *The Human Cycle,* 123.
17. Ignace Lepp, *The Psychology of Loving* (Baltimore: Helicon, 1963), 2.
18. Sri Aurobindo, *Thoughts and Aphorisms* (Pondicherry, India: Sri Aurobindo Ashram, 1982), 9.
19. In many ways, especially throughout *The Ascent of Mount Carmel,* Book II, in *The Collected Works of St. John of the Cross,* rev. ed., trans. Kieran Kavanaugh and Otilio Rodriguez (Washington, D.C.: Institute of Carmelite Studies, 1991).
20. Sri Aurobindo, *The Human Cycle,* 122.
21. John of the Cross, *The Ascent of Mount Carmel* II, 11:6, 16:10, 17:7.
22. A., ii, 190–193; also *Kesaputtiya Sutta,* A., i., 188.

23. Alan Watts, *The Wisdom of Insecurity* (New York: Pantheon Books, 1951), cited from paper edition (1968), 24.

24. Sri Aurobindo, *The Human Cycle*, 112.

25. John of the Cross, *The Ascent of Mount Carmel* II, 4:4.

26. Ibid.

27. Ibid., II, 12:3; III, 3:6.

28. Ibid., II, 4:4. Based on the original meanings of the word "*credo*" (see above p. 34), I am translating "*creyendo su ser*" differently than the translator I have been citing does.

29. Smith, *Faith and Belief*, 81. In *The Assurance of Things Hoped For: A Theology of Christian Faith* (New York: Oxford University Press, 1994), Avery Dulles disagrees with Smith's understanding of St. Thomas. I stand with Smith.

30. Ibid., 83.

31. Raymond Panikkar, "Faith — A Constitutive Dimension of Man," *Journal of Ecumenical Studies* 8 (1971): 223–54.

32. See *Summa Theologica* 2:2:1:3 (II:5–6)

33. Thich Nhat Hanh, *Interbeing: Commentaries on the Tiep Hien Precepts* (Berkeley, Calif.: Parallax Press, 1987), 27, 30, 32.

34. Smith, *Faith and Belief*, 40.

35. Ibid., 95.

36. Ibid., 96.

Chapter 6: Faith Is Not Feeling Sure

1. Etienne Gilson, *Elements of Christian Philosophy* (New York, 1960), 55.

2. Gordon Allport, *The Individual and His Religion* (New York: Macmillan, 1950), cited from paper edition (1960), 81.

3. Sarvepalli Radhakrishnan, *Recovery of Faith: The Way toward a Religion of the Spirit* (New York: Harper & Brothers, 1955), 191.

4. See Abraham Maslow, *Religions, Values, and Peak Experiences* (Columbus: Ohio State University Press, 1964).

5. John of the Cross, *The Ascent of Mount Carmel* II, 4:7 in *The Collected Works of St. John of the Cross*, rev. ed., trans. Kieran Kavanaugh and Otilio Rodriguez (Washington, D.C.: Institute of Carmelite Studies, 1991).

6. *Isa Upanishad*, 9. Vedanta is a reform of Hindu Vedic religion, believed to have been influenced in part by Buddhism. The Upanishads are the major scriptures that elaborate Vedantic understandings. They are considered to develop and complete the Vedas, Hinduism's ancient scriptures.

7. William James, "The Will to Believe," in William James, *The Will to Believe and Other Essays in Popular Philosophy* (New York: McKay, 1897), cited from John K. Roth, ed., *The Moral Philosophy of William James* (New York: Crowell, 1969), 203.

8. Article 157, p. 43.

9. Henry Fielding, *The History of Tom Jones: A Foundling* (New York: Random House, 1964), 69.

10. Abhishiktananda (Henri Le Saux), *The Farther Shore* (Delhi, India: ISPCK, 1975), 60.

11. Mary Jo Meadow and Richard D. Kahoe, *Psychology of Religion: Religion in Individual Lives* (New York: Harper & Row, 1984), chap. 25.

12. Allport, *The Individual and His Religion*, 78.

13. Eric Hoffer, *The True Believer* (New York: New American Library Mentor Book, 1951), 77, 79.

14. Ibid.

15. William James, *The Varieties of Religion Experience* (New York: McKay, 1902), cited from Collier Books edition (1961), 269.

16. Sigmund Freud, *The Future of an Illusion* (1927), trans. W. D. Robson-Scott (Garden City, N.Y.: Doubleday Anchor, 1961), 47.

17. G. K. Chesterton, *Orthodoxy* (New York: Image Books, 1959), 19.

18. Erich Fromm, *Psychoanalysis and Religion* (New Haven: Yale University Press, 1950), cited from Bantam edition (1967), 114.

19. Radhakrishnan, *Recovery of Faith*, 157.

20. David Bakan, *On Method: Toward a Reconstruction of Psychological Investigation* (San Francisco: Jossey-Bass, Inc., 1967), 154, 157.

21. John of the Cross, *The Ascent of Mount Carmel* III, 35: 7–8.

22. As explained by Sheikh Ragip of the Jerrahi Order of Sufis, Mankato, Minn., April 1993.

23. *Alagaddupamasutta, Majjhima-Nikaya.*

24. *Amritanada Upanishad* 1.

25. Sri Aurobindo Ghose, *The Synthesis of Yoga* (Pondicherry, India: Sri Aurobindo Ashram, 1976), 748.

26. Allport, *The Individual and His Religion*, 81.

27. See Alan Watts, *The Wisdom of Insecurity* (New York: Pantheon Books, 1951), paper edition (1968).

28. Allport, *The Individual and His Religion*, 81.

29. Watts, *The Wisdom of Insecurity*, 24.

Chapter 7: Faith Is Not Blind

1. Eric Hoffer, *The True Believer* (New York: New American Library Mentor Book, 1951), 75–76.

2. *Mahaparinibbana Sutta* I, 16–18. This story is also told in *Sampasadaniya Sutta* of *Digha Nikaya* and *Satipatthana Vagga* of *Samyutta Nikaya*.

3. *Tevijja Sutta*, from *Digha-Nikaya*, no. 13.

4. Paul Pruyser, *Between Belief and Unbelief* (New York: Harper & Row, 1974), 250.

5. Sarvepalli Radhakrishnan, *Recovery of Faith: The Way toward a Religion of the Spirit* (New York: Harper & Brothers, 1955), 191.

6. Sigmund Freud, *The Future of an Illusion* (1927), trans. and ed. James Strachey (New York: W. W. Norton, 1961), 26.

7. An early study affirming this, often repeated with the same results, is Stanley Milgram, "Group Pressure and Action against a Person," *Journal of Abnormal and Social Psychology* 69 (1964): 137–43.

8. Radhakrishnan, *Recovery of Faith*, 70.

9. John of the Cross, "Letter 24," in *The Collected Works of St. John of the Cross*, rev. ed., trans. Kieran Kavanaugh and Otilio Rodriguez (Washington, D.C.: Institute of Carmelite Studies, 1991), 759.

10. Hoffer, *The True Believer*, 78.

11. Ibid., 76.

12. Sri Aurobindo Ghose, *The Human Cycle, The Ideal of Human Unity, War and Self-Determination* (Pondicherry, India: Sri Aurobindo Ashram, 1971), 249.

13. Ibid., 32.

14. Luther, "Table Talk, Number 1687," in Frantz Funck-Brentano, *Luther* (London: Jonathan Cape, Ltd., 1939), 246.

15. The Index of Forbidden Books, now defunct, was a list of works that Catholics were forbidden to read. Reading them was considered a sufficiently serious sin to put one under threat of eternal damnation. These works were held to be detrimental to faith.

16. I admit to taking considerable unholy delight in the report a year later that this particular priest had "run off" to marry a church employee.

17. This is an actual case history from my internship in clinical psychology, with the targets of the man's voices changed to preserve confidentiality.

18. For discussion of this theme, see the work of orthodox Jewish psychologist David Bakan, *The Duality of Human Existence* (Chicago: Rand McNally & Co., 1966), 197–236.

19. Konrad Heiden, *Der Fuehrer* (Boston: Houghton Mifflin Company, 1944), 758.

20. See Susan Atkins, with Bob Slosser, *Child of Satan, Child of God* (Plainfield, N.J.: Logos International, 1977).

21. For full account of this now old story, see *Newsweek*, December 4, 1978, or *Time*, December 4, 1978.

22. Sri Aurobindo, *The Human Cycle*, 12.

23. Sri Aurobindo, *Essays on the Gita* (Pondicherry, India: Sri Aurobindo Ashram, 1972), 462–63; Radhakrishnan, *Recovery of Faith*, 8.

24. Radhakrishnan, *Recovery of Faith*, 8.

25. This word *shastra* can best be understood as the tradition taken as a whole.

26. Sri Aurobindo, *Essays on the Gita*, 462.

27. Sri Aurobindo, *The Human Cycle*, 13.

28. Ibid., 13

29. William James, *The Varieties of Religious Experience* (New York: McKay, 1902), cited from Collier Books edition (1961), 34.

30. Ibid., 33.

31. The hindrances are mental states that leave one agitated, disturbed, covetous, confused; they are called *kilesas*, or torments of the mind. They could be considered the "capital sins" in Buddhism.

32. *Milindapanha*, 51–62.

Chapter 8: Faith Is Not Narrow

1. William James, *The Varieties of Religious Experience* (New York: McKay, 1902), cited from Collier Books edition (1961), 281.

2. Sri Aurobindo Ghose, *Essays on the Gita* (Pondicherry, India: Sri Aurobindo Ashram, 1986), 465.

3. Robertson Davies, "A Few Kind Words for Superstition" *Newsweek*, November 20, 1978, 23.

4. Sarvepalli Radhakrishnan, *Recovery of Faith: The Way toward a Religion of the Spirit* (New York: Harper & Row, 1955), 70.

5. Father Wade, longtime chair of the Philosophy Department at St. Louis University.

6. The *I Ching* is the Chinese *Book of Changes*. One consults it as an oracle, tossing stones, coins, or dice to be directed to its appropriate passage to read. Traditionally, one prepared for such consultation for days by prayer, fasting, and vigils. Many Westerners have unfortunately and irreverently made a parlor game of it.

7. James, *The Varieties of Religious Experience*, 355.

8. R. W. Gleason, *The Search for God* (New York: Sheed & Ward, 1964), 14.

9. D. E. Trueblood, *The Logic of Belief* (New York: Harper & Row, 1942), 24.

10. Gordon Allport, "The Religious Context of Prejudice," *Journal for the Scientific Study of Religion*, 5 (1966): 447–57.

11. This first appeared in a very early issue of the *National Catholic Reporter* newspaper.

12. Paul Pruyser, *Between Belief and Unbelief* (New York: Harper & Row, 1974), 262.

13. Abraham Maslow, *Eupsychian Management* (Homewood Ill.: Irwin & Dorsey Press, 1965), 62.

14. Radhakrishnan, *Recovery of Faith*, 195.

15. Eric Hoffer, *The True Believer* (New York: New American Library Mentor Book, 1951), 81.

16. Mary Jo Meadow, "The Cross and the Seed: Active and Receptive Spiritualities," *Journal of Religion and Health* 17 (1978): 57–69.

17. Martin Marty, "Religious Cause, Religious Cure," *The Christian Century,* February 28, 1979, 213.

18. Radhakrishnan, *Recovery of Faith,* 70.

19. One can feel compassion for this woman in pain with intense self-hatred and hatred of femininity. Yet James's chapter-opening quote still holds.

20. Studies supporting this conclusion are cited in Mary Jo Meadow and Richard D. Kahoe, *Psychology of Religion: Religion in Individual Lives* (New York: Harper & Row, 1984), 22–23, 99–100.

21. James, *The Varieties of Religious Experience,* 271.

22. Ibid., 242.

23. Ann and Barry Ulanov, *Religion and the Unconscious* (Philadelphia: Westminster, 1975), 181.

24. Theodor Reik, "Masochism in Modern Man," in *Of Love and Lust* (New York: Farrar, Straus & Giroux, 1949), 242.

25. St. John of the Cross, *Ascent of Mount Carmel,* Books II and III, in *The Collected Works of St. John of the Cross,* rev. ed., trans. Kieran Kavanaugh and Otilio Rodriguez (Washington, D.C.: Institute of Carmelite Studies, 1991).

26. James, *The Varieties of Religious Experience,* 273.

Chapter 9: Faith Is Not Exclusive

1. Sarvepalli Radhakrishnan, *Recovery of Faith: The Way toward a Religion of the Spirit* (New York: Harper & Brothers, 1955), 157.

2. Ibid.

3. Abhishiktananda (Henri Le Saux), *The Farther Shore* (Delhi, India: ISPCK, 1975), 60.

4. From "Before a Collection Made for the Society for the Propagation of the Gospel," in *The Poetical Works of Reginald Heber, Late Lord Bishop of Calcutta* (New York: John W. Lovell Co., n.d., ca. 1842), 264–65.

5. *Nostra Aetate* (Declaration on the Relationship of the Church to Non-Christian Religions), no. 2; *Ad Gentes* (Decree on the Church's Missionary Activity), no. 18. These documents are explained more fully in Kevin Culligan, Mary Jo Meadow, and Daniel Chowning, *Purifying the Heart: Buddhist Insight Meditation for Christians* (New York: Crossroad, 1994), especially chap. 23.

6. Chwen Jiuan A. Lee and Thomas G. Hand, *A Taste of Water: Christianity through Taoist-Buddhist Eyes* (New York: Paulist Press, 1990), 10.

7. Wilfred Cantwell Smith, "Christian — Noun, or Adjective?" in *Questions of Religious Truth* (New York: Charles Scribner's Sons, 1967), 106.

8. Ibid., 122.

9. Lee and Hand, *A Taste of Water,* 10.

10. Aloysius Pieris, S.J., *Love Meets Wisdom: A Christian Experience of Buddhism* (Maryknoll, N.Y.: Orbis Books, 1988), 33.

11. Seiichi Yagi and Leonard Swidler, *A Bridge to Buddhist-Christian Dialogue* (New York: Paulist Press, 1990), 139. See also the discussion of *avatars* in chap. 4.

12. Ibid., 144.

13. Ibid.

14. Radhakrishnan, *Recovery of Faith*, 178–79.

15. See note 5 for this chapter.

16. *Contra Celsum*, IV, 16.

17. *II Sent.*, 3, 1, 1.

18. Pieris, *Love Meets Wisdom*, 23–24; emphasis in the original deleted.

19. Abhishiktananda, *Hindu-Christian Meeting Point: Within the Cave of the Heart* (Delhi, India: ISPCK, 1969), 113.

20. Ibid., 121.

21. Swami Sarananda, *Sri Sri Ramakrishna Lilaprasanga* (Calcutta: Ubhodhan Office, 1955), 335. Also in Swami Prabhavananda, *The Spiritual Heritage of India: A Clear Summary of Indian Philosophy and Religion* (Hollywood, Calif.: Vedanta Press, 1979), 340.

22. Swami Nikhilananda, trans., *The Gospel of Sri Ramakrishna* (New York: Ramakrishna-Vivekananda Center, 1952), 35.

23. Yagi and Swidler, *A Bridge to Buddhist-Christian Dialogue*, 3, 6.

24. These scriptures form the basis of Vedantic understandings.

25. Abhishiktananda, *The Farther Shore*, 61.

26. Abhishiktananda, *Hindu-Christian Meeting Point*, 96.

27. Ibid., 105.

28. Krishna in *Bhagavad-Gita* IV: 11, "As people approach me so do I accept them. Those on all sides follow my path."

29. Radhakrishnan, *Recovery of Faith*, 155.

30. Ibid., 155–56.

31. Ibid., 199.

32. Nicholas de Cusa, "De Pace Seu Concordantia Fidei," I, 1, in Raimundo Panikkar, *The Intrareligious Dialogue* (New York: Paulist Press, 1978), xi.

33. Ramon Lull, *Obres Essencials*, vol. 1 (Barcelona: Editorial selecta, 1957), 1138, in Panikkar, *The Intrareligious Dialogue*, xiii.

34. William Law, "The Spirit of Prayer" (1749), in *Complete Works of William Law*, vol. 7 (London, 1762).

35. Nicolai Berdyaev, *Faiths and Fellowship*, 1936, 79.

36. Panikkar, *The Intrareligious Dialogue*, 2.

37. This statement uses successively a Christian, Buddhist, and Vedantic way of wording the essential truth of our oneness with each other.

38. I first saw this notion of "the common enemy" articulated by Karl Menninger in the *Bulletin of the Menninger Clinic* 25 (1961): 277–89.

Chapter 10: Faith Is a Choice

1. Dag Hammarskjöld, *Markings*, trans. Leif Sjoberg and W. H. Auden (New York: Alfred A. Knopf, 1965), 205.

2. R. B. Perry, *The Thought and Character of William James* (briefer version) (Cambridge: Harvard University Press, 1948), 121.

3. William James, "The Will to Believe," in William James, *The Will to Believe and Other Essays in Popular Philosophy* (New York: McKay, 1897), cited from John K. Roth, ed., *The Moral Philosophy of William James* (New York Crowell, 1969).

4. James, "The Will to Believe," *passim*.

5. Erik Erikson, *Childhood and Society*, 2nd ed. (New York: Norton, 1963), 250.

6. Erik Erikson, *Toys and Reason: Stages in the Ritualization of Experience* (New York: Norton, 1977).

7. Paul Pruyser, "Psychological Roots and Branches of Belief," *Pastoral Psychology* 28 (1979): 11.

8. William James, *The Principles of Psychology* (New York: Holt, Rinehart & Winston, 1890), cited from R. M. Hutchins, ed., *Great Books of the Western World* (Chicago: Encyclopaedia Britannica, 1952), volume 53: *William James*, 661.

9. *Kesaputtiya Sutta*, A. 1., 188 (to Kalamas).

10. James, "The Will to Believe," 209.

11. Sri Aurobindo, *Essays on the Gita* (Pondicherry, India: Sri Aurobindo Ashram, 1972), 465–66.

12. Ibid.

13. James, "The Will to Believe," 212–13.

14. Wilfred Cantwell Smith, *Faith and Belief* (Princeton, N.J.: Princeton University Press, 1979), 59; emphasis in original.

15. Wilfred Cantwell Smith, *Questions of Religious Truth* (New York: Charles Scribner's Sons, 1967), 43–44.

16. Ibid., 51–52.

17. Sri Aurobindo, *The Mother* (Pondicherry, India: Sri Aurobindo Ashram Trust, 1972), 16.

18. W. B. Cannon, *The Wisdom of the Body* (New York: Norton, 1932).

19. Jerome Frank, *Persuasion and Healing* (Baltimore: Johns Hopkins University Press, 1961), 60–61.

20. There are accounts of this in Matthew 13:58 and Mark 6:5, 6.

21. I am told that this story appeared in an issue of *Fellowship in Prayer* magazine.

Chapter 11: Faith Is a Confident Experiment

1. Paul Tillich, *Biblical Wisdom and the Search for Ultimate Reality* (Chicago: University of Chicago Press, 1955), 53.

2. *Ariyapariyesana Sutta, Majjhima Nikaya, Sutta* no. 26.

3. Wilfred Cantwell Smith, *Faith and Belief* (Princeton, N.J.: Princeton University Press, 1979), 64; emphasis in the original.

4. Exact source unknown; the translation is that of Wilfred Cantwell Smith.

5. Seshagiri Rao, *The Concept of Shraddha (in the Brahmanas, Upanishads and the Gita)* (Patiala: Roy, 1971), 162–63.

6. From a talk given at Insight Meditation Society, Barre, Mass., by Steven Smith, October 3, 1994. U Pandita is also one of the author's Buddhist teachers.

7. John of the Cross, *The Ascent of Mount Carmel* II, 9:1, in *The Collected Works of St. John of the Cross*, rev. ed., trans. Kieran Kavanaugh and Otilio Rodriguez (Washington, D.C.: Institute of Carmelite Studies, 1991).

8. Smith, *Faith and Belief*, 67.

9. Ibid., 68.

10. Ibid., 103.

11. Sri Aurobindo Ghose, *Essays on the Gita* (Pondicherry, India: Sri Aurobindo Ashram, 1972), 295.

12. Ibid., 475.

13. Ibid., 195.

14. *Suttanipata* 1146.

15. See, for example, Matthew 9:22; Mark 5:34, 10:52; Luke 8:48, 18:42.

16. Sri Aurobindo, *Essays on the Gita*, 296.

17. *The Cloud of Unknowing*, ed. James Walsh (New York: Paulist Press, 1981), 138–39.

18. John of the Cross, *The Spiritual Canticle*, 12:4, in Kavanaugh and Rodriguez.

19. David Bakan, *On Method: Toward a Reconstruction of Psychological Investigation* (San Francisco: Jossey-Bass, 1967), 156–57.

20. *Kesaputtiya Sutta*, A. 1., 188 (to Kalamas).

21. Raimundo Panikkar, *The Intrareligious Dialogue* (New York: Paulist Press, 1978), 22.

22. Sri Aurobindo, *The Human Cycle, The Ideal of Human Unity, War and Self-Determination* (Pondicherry, India: Sri Aurobindo Ashram, 1971), 249.

23. Abhishiktananda (Henri Le Saux), *Saccidananda: A Christian Approach to Advaitic Experience* (Delhi, India: ISPCK, 1984), 72.

24. Smith, *Faith and Belief*, 64.

25. Ramanuja, in A. Govindacharya, trans., *Sri Bhagavad-Gita with Sri Ramanujacharya's Vishishtadvaita Commentary, Translated into English* (Madras: Vaijayanti Press, 1989), 17:2, 502.

26. Paul Pruyser, "Phenomenology and Dynamics of Hoping," *Journal for the Scientific Study of Religion* 3 (1963): 94.

27. Raimundo Panikkar, *The Intrareligious Dialogue* (New York: Paulist Press, 1978), 13.

28. Søren Kierkegaard, *The Journals of Kierkegaard* (New York: Harper & Row, 1959), 184–85.

29. Sarvepalli Radhakrishnan, *The Principal Upanishads, Edited with Introduction, Text, Translation and Notes* (London: Allen & Unwin, 1953), 595.

30. Sri Aurobindo, *The Synthesis of Yoga* (Pondicherry, India: Sri Aurobindo Ashram, 1976), 743.

31. Smith, *Faith and Belief,* 61.

32. Ibid., 63; emphasis in original.

33. Sri Aurobindo, *Essays on the Gita,* 475.

34. Smith, *Faith and Belief,* 64.

35. Ibid., 63.

36. Abhishiktananda, *The Farther Shore* (Delhi, India: ISPCK, 1975), 60.

37. Smith, *Faith and Belief,* 54.

38. Sri Aurobindo, *The Synthesis of Yoga,* 746.

39. Smith, *Faith and Belief,* 42; emphasis in original.

40. Sri Aurobindo, *Essays on the Gita,* 461–62.

41. See note 16 in chapter 1 for explanation of the word *Dhamma.*

42. Sri Aurobindo, *Essays on the Gita,* 464.

Chapter 12: Faith Is Sometimes Difficult

1. Søren Kierkegaard, *The Journals of Kierkegaard* (New York: Harper & Row, 1959), 68.

2. Peter Shaffer, *Equus* (New York: Penguin Books, 1977), 80. This play makes a powerful statement about spiritual yearning.

3. Sri Aurobindo Ghose, *The Synthesis of Yoga* (Pondicherry, India: Sri Aurobindo Ashram, 1976), 750.

4. Alfred, Lord Tennyson, "In Memoriam" (1896).

5. For example, see Mary Jo Meadow and Richard D. Kahoe, *Psychology of Religion: Religion in Individual Lives* (New York: Harper & Row, 1984), 259. See also H. D. Rumke, *The Psychology of Unbelief* (New York: Sheed & Ward, 1962).

6. Paul Pruyser, *Between Belief and Unbelief* (New York: Harper & Row, 1974), 63.

7. Sri Aurobindo, *The Synthesis of Yoga,* 744.

8. Paul Tillich, *The Dynamics of Faith* (New York: Harper & Brothers, 1957), 73.

9. Ibid., 134.

10. Gordon Allport, *The Individual and His Religion* (New York: Macmillan, 1950), chap. 5.

11. J. B. Phillips, *Your God Is Too Small* (New York: Macmillan Co., 1953), 58.

12. The word *shastra* is best understood as the tradition in its totality: beliefs, practices, morality, and so on.

13. Sri Aurobindo, *Essays on the Gita* (Pondicherry, India: Sri Aurobindo Ashram, 1972), 463.

14. This presentation on agnosticism is drawn from Paul Pruyser, *Between Belief and Unbelief* (New York: Harper & Row, 1974), 155–56.

15. Pruyser, *Between Belief and Unbelief*, 248.

16. Ibid., 60.

17. Ibid., 61.

18. Ibid., 61–62.

19. Robert Morhaus, in a talk given at Insight Meditation Society, Barre, Mass., December 1986.

20. Sri Aurobindo, *The Synthesis of Yoga*, 745.

21. Dag Hammarskjöld, *Markings*, trans. Leif Sjoberg and W. H. Auden (New York: Alfred A. Knopf, 1965), 16.

22. Sri Aurobindo, *The Synthesis of Yoga*, 749.

23. Allport, *The Individual and His Religion*, cited from paper edition (1960), 81.

24. Raimundo Panikkar, *The Intrareligious Dialogue* (New York: Paulist Press, 1978), 19.

25. Orlo Strunk, *Mature Religion: A Psychological Study* (New York: Abingdon, 1965).

26. Gordon Allport, *Personality: A Psychological Interpretation* (New York: Holt, Rinehart and Winston, 1937).

27. Gordon Allport, "Mental Health: A Generic Attitude," *Journal of Religion and Health* 4 (1964): 16.

28. Allport, *The Individual and His Religion*, 68–69.

29. Sri Aurobindo, *Essays on the Gita*, 195.

30. Allport, *The Individual and His Religion*, 137.

Chapter 13: Faith Is a Darkness

1. I read this years ago and have been unable to relocate the reference. I think the author was French.

2. J. A. T. Robinson, *Honest to God* (Philadelphia: Westminster, 1963), 124.

3. *Stromata*, I, 2, V, 12.

4. John of the Cross, *The Ascent of Mount Carmel*, I, 13:11, in *The Collected Works of St. John of the Cross*, rev. ed., trans. Kieran Kavanaugh and Otilio Rodriguez (Washington, D.C.: Institute of Carmelite Studies, 1991).

5. Wilfred Cantwell Smith, *Faith and Belief* (Princeton, N.J.: Princeton University Press, 1979), 131.

6. Ibid., 27ff.

7. Leslie Dewart, *The Future of Belief: Theism in a World Come of Age* (New York: Herder & Herder, 1966), 168.

8. John of the Cross, *The Dark Night*, II, 3:3, in Kavanaugh and Rodriguez.

9. Ibid., II, 9:4.

10. Smith, *Faith and Belief*, 133.

11. *Kena Upanishad*, II,3.

12. Meister Eckhart, "Sermon IV: The Feast of the Holy Trinity," in *Meister Eckhart: Teacher and Preacher*, ed. Bernard McGinn (New York: Paulist Press, 1986), 210–11.

13. Sri Aurobindo Ghose, *Essays on the Gita* (Pondicherry, India: Sri Aurobindo Ashram, 1972), 324. *Neti, neti* means "not this, not this;" one goes through every possible object negating it thus.

14. Sarvepalli Radhakrishnan, *Recovery of Faith: The Way toward a Religion of the Spirit* (New York: Harper & Brothers, 1955), 154.

15. St. John's teachings on faith are mainly in Book II of *The Ascent of Mount Carmel.*

16. John of the Cross, *The Ascent of Mount Carmel* II, 6:2.

17. Ibid., II, 10:4.

18. Ibid., II, 3:4.

19. For a good discussion of this, see Sri Aurobindo, *The Life Divine* (Pondicherry, India: Sri Aurobindo Ashram, 1973), 47.

20. Sri Aurobindo, *The Synthesis of Yoga* (Pondicherry, India: Sri Aurobindo Ashram, 1976), 747.

21. Sri Aurobindo, *The Life Divine,* 53.

22. Sri Aurobindo, *The Synthesis of Yoga,* 745.

23. Ibid., 746.

24. John of the Cross, *The Ascent of Mount Carmel,* II, 3:1.

25. Ibid., III, 32:4.

26. John of the Cross, *The Living Flame of Love,* 1:20, in Kavanaugh and Rodriguez.

27. John of the Cross, *The Spiritual Canticle,* 12:2, in Kavanaugh and Rodriguez.

28. This is discussed beautifully in Pseudo-Dionysius, *Mystical Theology,* II.

29. Pseudo-Dionysius, *Letters,* V.

30. *De Potentia,* VII, 5, ad. 14.

31. The *Tao Te Ching* is available in many translations and editions.

32. Sri Aurobindo, *The Life Divine*, 49. Hindu Vedanta speaks of the Ultimate Reality as being (*sat*), consciousness (*chit*), and bliss (*ananda*): *Sachchidananda*.

33. *Enneads*, V.3.17.

34. See John of the Cross, *The Ascent of Mount Carmel*, II:7, for a discussion of what he means by this.

35. Pascal Kaplan, "A conversation with Murshida Ivy O. Duce," *Re-Vision* 1 (1978): 38.

36. Sri Aurobindo, *The Human Cycle, The Ideal of Human Unity, War and Self-Determination* (Pondicherry, India: Sri Aurobindo Ashram, 1971), 126.

37. Psychologist Gordon Allport discussed this criterion and others for personal maturity in a psychology classic, *Personality: A Psychological Interpretation* (New York: Holt, Rinehart and Winston, 1937).

38. Sri Aurobindo, *The Synthesis of Yoga*, 747–48.

39. Paul Pruyser, *Between Belief and Unbelief* (New York: Harper & Row, 1974), 62.

40. Peter Bertocci, *Religion As Creative Insecurity* (New York: Association Press, 1958), 14.

41. Dietrich Bonhoeffer, *Letters and Papers from Prison* (London: SCM Press, 1953), 122.

42. Sri Aurobindo, *The Synthesis of Yoga*, 744.

43. Nyanatiloka, *Path to Deliverance* (Kandy, Sri Lanka: Buddhist Publication Society, 1951/1982), 181.

44. John of the Cross, *The Dark Night*, II, 8:5.

Chapter 14: Faith Is a Dynamic Process

1. Sri Aurobindo Ghose, *The Synthesis of Yoga* (Pondicherry, India: Sri Aurobindo Ashram, 1976), 77.

2. Bhoga, in Swami Prabhavananda, *The Spiritual Heritage of India: A Clear Summary of Indian Philosophy and Religion* (Hollywood, Calif.: Vedanta Press, 1979), 239.

3. *Sutta-nipata*, 182–84.

4. Asvaghosha, *The Awakening of Faith in the Great Source of All* (ca. 75 B.C.E.–80 C.E., various editions).

5. James Fowler, *Stages of Faith: The Psychology of Human Development and The Quest for Meaning* (New York: Harper & Row, 1981).

6. Gordon Allport, *The Individual and His Religion* (New York: Macmillan, 1950), cited from paper edition (1960), 33.

7. *Majjhima-nikaya* I, 36–38 (*Vatthupama Sutta*).

8. Thérèse of Lisieux, *Story of a Soul* (Washington, D.C.: Institute of Carmelite Studies, 1975).

9. John of the Cross, *The Ascent of Mount Carmel*, II, 9:1, in *The Collected Works of St. John of the Cross*, rev. ed., trans. Kieran Kavanaugh and Otilio Rodriguez (Washington, D.C.: Institute of Carmelite Studies, 1991). To avoid confusion, I have retranslated the parts in the brackets differently than the source cited translates them.

10. Ibid., I, 2:3.

11. Sri Aurobindo, *Essays on the Gita* (Pondicherry, India: Sri Aurobindo Ashram, 1972), 464.

12. Ibid., 273.

13. Sri Aurobindo, *The Synthesis of Yoga*, 233.

14. *Indriya-Samyutta*, Sutta 50, PTS: iv, 225 ff.; *Samyutta Nikaya* Kindred Sayings.

15. *Ishwara* is God seen as personal being in Hindu traditions. They also commonly consider God in the impersonal guise of the *Brahman*.

16. Sri Aurobindo, *The Synthesis of Yoga*, 753.

17. Sri Aurobindo, *Essays on the Gita*, 467.

18. Dag Hammarskjöld, *Markings*, trans. Leif Sjoberg and W. H. Auden (New York: Alfred A. Knopf, 1965), 16.

19. *Sermo* 43, 7, 9.

Postscript

1. Wilfred Cantwell Smith, *Faith and Belief* (Princeton, N.J.: Princeton University Press, 1979), 124.

2. Lama Anagarika Govinda, *The Psychological Attitude of Early Buddhist Philosophy and Its Systematic Representation according to Abhidhamma Tradition* (New York: Samuel Weiser, 1974), 41–42.

3. Swami Prabhavananda, *The Spiritual Heritage of India: A Clear Summary of Indian Philosophy and Religion* (Hollywood, Calif.: Vedanta Press, 1979), 20.

4. Jacques Maritain, *Degrees of Knowledge* (New York: Scribner, 1918).

5. We find the promise of this in the Mahayana Buddhist *Sad-dharma Pundarika*, IV, and in the Hindu *Bhagavad Gita*, IV:8.